How to
Write Bids that
Win Business

How to Write Bids that Win Business

A guide to improving your bidding
success rate and winning more tenders

**Martyn Curley, David Molian
and Stephen Oldbury**

Hh

HARRIMAN HOUSE LTD
18 College Street
Petersfield
Hampshire
GU31 4AD
GREAT BRITAIN
Tel: +44 (0)1730 233870
Email: enquiries@harriman-house.com
Website: www.harriman-house.com

First published in Great Britain in 2018
Copyright © Martyn Curley, David Molian and Stephen Oldbury

The right of Martyn Curley, David Molian and Stephen Oldbury to be identified as the Authors
has been asserted in accordance with the Copyright, Design and Patents Act 1988.

Hardback ISBN: 978-0-85719-653-8
eBook ISBN: 978-0-85719-654-5

British Library Cataloguing in Publication Data
A CIP catalogue record for this book can be obtained from the British Library.

Contents

Part III – Review and Improve

Part IV – A Glimpse of the Future

Appendices

About the Authors

David Molian

David Molian is a commercial writer and educator, who has served on the faculties of Imperial College Business School and Cranfield School of Management. For many years he was Director of Cranfield's prestigious Business Growth Programme and post-retirement remains a Cranfield Visiting Fellow. He has personally founded or co-founded three businesses and has advised numerous business owners on growth strategies for their companies. He is the author/co-author of several books and award-winning case studies on such businesses as Hotel Chocolat, Cobra Beer and GoApe, and has contributed features and commentary to the *Financial Times*, the *Daily Telegraph* and *Director* magazine. He contributes a monthly column to the website Fresh Business Thinking, is a Criticaleye Thought Leader and a co-founder of the Bid Writing Academy. He is a graduate of the University of Oxford.

Martyn Curley and Steve Oldbury

Martyn Curley FIoD and Steve Oldbury FRICS are co-founders of Bidwriting.com, a specialist bid writing consultancy that works in 35 market sectors. It was established ten years ago. The founders, at that time directors of a FTSE 250 company, spotted a gap in the market when they were bidding multi-million pound projects in the public and private sectors. They developed the business via Cranfield University's Business Growth Programme and achieved Investors in People 'Gold'

Accreditation. The company is consultant to some of the UK's and Europe's largest organisations. Martyn and Steve are co-founders of the Bid Writing Academy.

Acknowledgements

A number of individuals and organisations have assisted us in researching and writing this book. We would like to record our thanks to the following:

➤ John Algar, Senior Lecturer in Project and Programme Management, Cranfield School of Management, and all-round contracts guru.

➤ Gus Tugendhat and Ben Rycroft of Tussell, leading analysts and aggregators of UK public sector tender data (www.tussell.com).

➤ The Bid Writing A-Team, in particular for their diligent reading of early drafts of this book and their invaluable insights and comments.

➤ Craig Pearce, Senior Commissioning Editor at Harriman House, for his encouragement and support.

Any remaining errors or omissions are the responsibility of the authors.

Preface

Most companies would love to win business *without* having to go through a formal procurement process. Some will do almost anything to avoid this, seeking to build their organisation based on direct relationships with customers or clients. But in many business-to-business markets it's just not possible to secure work without bidding for it. The pressure to put projects out for tender is coming from all directions: from government, in the form of streamlining public expenditure, to demonstrate a fair and open process and securing value for the taxpayer; and in the private sector, to minimise costs and show value for money for shareholders.

This trend has increased over the last 30 years and is only going to continue to grow. Across the world, thousands of billions of dollars, pounds, euros, renminbi, yen, and virtually every other currency you can think of, are now spent annually on projects competed for by bidding organisations. In the UK alone, the government spent £232 billion on procurement in 2016, virtually all of it on work won by open tendering. In the United States, the equivalent figure for federal government expenditure exceeds $1 trillion – and that takes no account of what is spent at the level of individual states. Our own research based on publicly available data gives the following league table of procurement spend.

Table 1: Annual public procurement spend by country/ trading bloc

Rank	Country	US$ bn
1	USA	19,377.2
2	EU [27 countries, excluding UK]	14,360.1
3	China [excluding Hong Kong]	12,362.0
4	Japan	5,106.0
5	UK	2,609.9
6	India	2,458.0
7	Canada	1,672.3
8	Russia	1,442.0
9	Australia	1,344.0
10	Turkey	770.0
11	Saudi Arabia	689.0
12	Switzerland	684.0
13	Arab Emirates [excluding Qatar and Kuwait]	408.0
14	Norway	393.0
15	Hong Kong	326.0
16	New Zealand	193.0
17	Qatar	171.0
18	Kuwait	125.0
19	Iceland	21.4

Source : IMF World Economic Outlook 2016: Projections for 2017.

Collectively this amounts to over $60 trillion of public expenditure, *per year*. It's an interesting mix, split roughly 50/50 between developed and developing countries. For instance, in May 2017 the state-owned China Development Bank announced it had set aside almost $900bn for more than 900 projects to support its One Belt, One Road project. The grand vision is to recreate the ancient Silk Road linking trade between East and West through improved road and rail links, and much of the financing will be managed by the City of London. The potential bidding opportunities for British architects, consulting and civil engineers are enormous. Later in the book we explore how such international projects align with the comparative ease of doing business in different nations.

By anyone's standards $60 trillion is a big number. We figure that *between six and seven million people* worldwide are involved every year in writing and submitting bids. The number of bids submitted globally each year is probably – and this is our best guess – in excess of 100m. We've been in the bidding business a long time, and even we are overawed by the sheer size of the market when we look at the data.

Yet even these numbers underestimate the scale of bidding activity, since official statistics don't capture work which is put out for tender by private businesses, unrelated to public procurement contracts. If, for example, an oil major invites tenders to commission or decommission a rig, the awarded contract will remain commercially confidential. Such bid-for work, carried out purely in the private sector without any element of public funding, is almost certainly smaller in value and volume than public procurement, but it's unquestionably worth many billions of pounds every year.

In short, there's never been a more exciting time to be bidding for projects.

Your mind may well be starting to boggle at these global figures, so let's illustrate the point with a specific and familiar example of which we have direct experience: the tendering cycle for the construction and management of a typical new school in the UK. To get the building up and ready to use, approximately 100 bids will be submitted, with the same number of teams behind them. If the average number of people per team is three, that's 300 people involved in competing to win both the main contract, and the numerous sub-contract elements that will deliver the project.

Once it's completed, we need to fill the building and start operating. If the school is to be run as an Academy, as most now are, under contract to a non-government body, as many as 50 bids could be submitted. Before the doors are open for business, 50 bidding teams and perhaps a further 150 people will be involved. From start to finish through the life of the project, 150[1] bids could be submitted, requiring input from 450 people. In Part I we walk through such a project in detail, to explain how the numbers are arrived at. That's just one project – and hundreds of new schools are constructed in the UK every year, many of them under a nationally mandated framework.

Competing to win

Given the pervasive nature of bidding across so many commercial sectors, this leaves business-to-business firms with two basic choices. Either avoid having to tender for jobs wherever you can, which is increasingly difficult in many markets. Or become reconciled to this growing fact of life and become good at it, or even better than you already are. Indeed, embrace it, and view it as your competitive advantage. We're going to show you why option two makes good commercial sense.

In this book we feature an imaginary business. Imaginary, yes, but representative of the many client companies that we've worked with for over a decade. We'll explain how putting into practice, step by step, the tactics and techniques we've developed can transform this business's bid writing performance. Through upgrading its ability to win bids, the business will improve its top-line revenues, reduce its costs, make more money and be an all-round happier place to work. It is, if you like, a live case study. We focus just on that part of the business which makes its living from bidding successfully and show in detail the impact of more than doubling an industry-average success rate of 12.5%. We know, because we've seen numerous businesses do this.

---

[1] At an average of 30 per tender. In fact we think this is a conservative estimate. In a series of bids we recently advised on, bidders per tender ranged in number from 185 to 33.

Three key points about bids that win business

We've observed three key features that appear consistently in successful bids. They are the vital ingredients that combine to capture the reader's attention and catapult the bid to the top of the pile.

1. **First, they sell**. A successful bid is, above all, a sales document. It sells your business as a supplier, it sells your experience and expertise, and it sells your people as the right team to deliver the project on specification, to budget and on time.

2. **Second, they tell a compelling and convincing story**. A winning submission contains a narrative that the reader can easily follow, can pick up and can return to seamlessly.

3. **And third, a winning bid avoids the basic errors** which at the outset eliminate also-rans from serious consideration.

In this book we show how you can do these three things and, by doing so, load the dice in your favour.

Why we wrote this book

How To Write Bids That Win Business has essentially three types of content: tips, techniques and tactics. In Part I, for example, we outline our tips for spotting at the early stage the tenders that you definitely *don't* want to win, as they are likely only to cause you grief and cost you money. If they're not worth winning, you don't want to waste your time on losing propositions, but to focus your attention on the bids you really *do* want to win.

In Part II, we discuss the often-overlooked techniques of story-telling and how these can be employed to engage your reader and thus create a compelling bid.

In Part III we show you how to make tactical preparations that ensure you make the best possible impression at a shortlister interview. And that's just a sample of the practical guidance with which we have filled this book.

Our aim, then, was not to write yet another compliance guide, of which a number already exist. Instead, there are three main reasons why we decided to write this book.

First, we are passionate about writing *bids that win business*. Between us we have over 30 years' experience of bid writing consultancy. Having cut our teeth working on bids as employees of other companies, in 2006 we set up Bidwriting.com to specialise in doing just that for ourselves. In the years since we started, we've worked for dozens of clients bidding for projects all across the world. Many are famous names that you would recognise instantly if client confidentiality didn't stop us naming them! We started the business with enthusiasm. Today, we are if anything even more enthusiastic, because we've seen the dramatic difference that better bid writing performance makes. That difference finds expression not just in improved top line and bottom line results for organisations, but in people's lives and careers. The impacts that we've seen make us more than enthusiasts – we're unashamedly advocates and cheerleaders for better bid writing. We believe that bid writing is still hugely undervalued as a key business skill and we hope that sharing what we've learned over the years will help change that perception.

Second, this book is also meant as something of an antidote. The world is drowning in books by management gurus, promising a better business and, not infrequently, a better life. Every few years a new silver bullet is fired: if it's not quality circles, it's business process mapping, or business transformation, or systems thinking or blue ocean strategy. Downsize, upsize, rightsize. The list goes on and on. Virtually every month another celebrity businessman and woman shares the secrets of their success. We're not denying that the theories and ideas presented provide insight, inspiration and food for thought. The search for business improvement is, or should be, a never-ending journey. But we're sceptical about anything that's packaged as "the answer", if only because business is inherently complicated. One size seldom fits all and, like everything in life, companies are subject to reversals of fortune. Businesses that one moment are held up as exemplars the next minute fall from grace. [In fact, featuring in this type of literature seems to have jinxed the fortunes of many a corporate giant, IBM and Hewlett-Packard to name but two.]

There is also often a yawning gap between theory and execution. We've come away from the guru literature too often thinking "that's all very well, but how do I actually implement this stuff?" We're sure that many of you reading this have experienced the same reaction. So if you're expecting a management panacea, you'll be disappointed. This book makes no claims to be a magic bullet – but it could seriously improve your organisation's performance.

And this brings us on to the third reason for writing this book. **We want to seriously improve your organisation's performance**, through practical, meat-and-potatoes advice: things that you can actually put into practice that will make a tangible difference. These actions don't require a radical restructuring of the entire organisation, the hiring of expensive consultants, or a subscription to a set of videos or online tutorials. We'll be showing you changes that you can introduce tomorrow, at minimal expense, as well as changes in mindset and processes that will yield longer-term benefits.

In summary, the main aims of this book are to enable you to:

- Create a comprehensive bid writing strategy.
- Increase your bid writing success rate.
- Avoid the common mistakes made by most bidders.
- Identify and steer clear of loss-making projects.
- Embed continuous improvement in your bidding function.
- Increase your organisation's profits.

The audience

Our book is aimed at two kinds of reader, and is designed to work equally well for both.

First, it's aimed at the partner or director responsible and accountable for the organisation's bid writing strategy and activity. He or she may well not be involved in the day-to-day process of preparing and submitting bids – they may not even understand it in detail, having received no formal training. But by improving their knowledge, they will be able to provide the supporting structures and processes that enable the organisation's bid writers to produce their best work. And that will translate into a more profitable organisation, a less stressful working environment and better staff retention.

The second audience is those at the coalface, the people whose day job is writing the bids that win business and pay people's salaries. It's a huge responsibility and is often not accorded the respect we believe it deserves. Historically most bid writers find themselves doing the job more or less by accident, having started their business life in a function such as Administration, Sales or Marketing. Their talent for writing bids emerges in the course of their career and they learn their craft by working on the job. So do other commercial writers such as advertising copywriters and journalists. But unlike these professions, bid writing has generally lacked a career path, clearly-defined professional development and external accreditation. As a result, even bid writers of long-standing often have gaps in their knowledge. This book will, we hope, address those gaps and refresh both their professional understanding and enthusiasm for their work.

Design of the book

This book is structured in a way that reflects the natural bid writing cycle: Preparation, Creation, Review and Submission, and Post-Bid Review. These are covered in Parts I to III. In a final section, Part IV, we put forward our views on future trends and new developments that will affect the principles and practice of bid writing, and describe what it will take to stand out as a winner in this emergent new world.

At the back of the book you will also find a number of appendices. Appendices 1–3 expand on information featured in Parts I–IV, and are clearly flagged up in the text. Appendix 1 explains how we calculate our estimate of bid volumes, and supplies our full Bid/No Bid screening template. Appendix 2 provides a comprehensive checklist for use prior to submitting a bid, and a fuller version of the BAFO [Best and Final Offer] case study described in Part II. Appendix 3 outlines the requirements of the GDPR [General Data Protection Regulation] which comes into force in May 2018, with which contractors must comply.

Appendix 4 is a review of the lessons to be learned from the collapse in January 2018 of the UK's second-largest public-sector contractor, Carillion. This debacle vividly reinforces some of the key themes of this book, and we were keen to capture these lessons while these events were still current.

How to use this book

Research suggests that, when presented with a new idea or information, people tend broadly to fall into two camps: those who believe it when they see it, and those who see it when they believe it. If this distinction seems a little mysterious, consider how you approach the assembly and completion of a jigsaw puzzle. Some people focus on fitting the component parts together, usually working from the margins towards the centre, allowing the picture to emerge progressively. At a certain point, when they see enough of the picture, they are confident they are on the right track: they *believe* it. Others start by fixing the completed puzzle in their mind, or referring to the picture on the box, and reverting to it continuously in the process of assembly. By envisaging the end state from the start, they are confident in the process. Each approach is equally valid and likely to lead to successful completion of the puzzle.

The divergence reflects different preferences in styles of thinking and processing of information.[2]

We cannot predict the preferred thinking style of readers, so we suggest that you read this book initially all the way through, to gain an overview. We have done our best to write in a tight and direct manner, so that the ideas presented can be rapidly assimilated. When you have had the opportunity to digest the contents, you will be best placed to decide how to implement the guidance and suggestions inside your own organisation.

Glossary of terms

BAFO: Best and Final Offer

ITT: Invitation to tender

PQQ: Preliminary qualification questionnaire

PRQ: Preliminary request for quotations

RFP: Request for proposals

RFQ: Request for quotations

RFT: Request for tender [an invitation to bid]

---

[2]   We are indebted to Ron Young of Knowledge Associates for this insight.

PART I

PREPARATION

Introduction

PERFECT PREPARATION PREVENTS poor performance. The converse of this old management rule of thumb is that imperfect preparation produces substandard performance, or at the very least leaves you at the mercy of events. Very few businesses grow and prosper by accident, and if your success largely depends on your ability to win work through bidding you can't rely on getting lucky. Yet we have been constantly surprised by how many organisations that apply rigorous planning elsewhere in their business fail to adopt a disciplined approach to their bidding.

Part I starts by walking through a typical bidding *supply chain*. Even in large organisations, bid writers and bid managers often have a limited idea of the bigger picture. They understand who their immediate clients and suppliers are, but don't really grasp where they sit within the scheme of things.

The fact is that very few bids happen within a vacuum and to understand the context and what is driving the process helps to produce a better and more compelling bid. Understanding the bidding supply chain will also help you to appreciate the varying chances of success as the bidding chain progresses through its life cycle. At every stage there's an opportunity to beat the odds by avoiding the common errors that eliminate many bids early on.

The focus then turns to how to create a bid writing strategy that harnesses your strengths and builds on your organisation's track record. The fact that so many organisations have no effective bid writing strategy creates huge opportunities for those that do. We show how taking some fairly simple steps can have a dramatic effect on an organisation's performance, and outline the tangible and less tangible benefits that result. Two steps that produce maximum impact are linking your bid writing strategy to the Sales and Marketing functions, and setting improvement goals. Sales and Marketing can provide you with invaluable broad and specific market intelligence, informing your strategy and checking its validity. Measurable improvement in your bidding performance translates into better margins and improved morale, as the sense of winning spreads through the organisation.

Successful strategy is equally about what you choose *not* to do. Some bids should be avoided at all costs. Either they're taking you in the wrong direction or they're a poor match with your organisation's capabilities. If you're unfortunate enough to win them, the chances are that you'll lose money and be burdened with what we term the winner's curse. We profile the warning signs and share with you our Bid/No Bid template that helps to screen out the losing propositions at the outset, leaving you to concentrate on bids you have a better chance of winning. If the potential opportunity passes the screening, there are certain key questions you need to answer to ensure that you are fully equipped to enter the contest: in our words, *preparing for battle*.

Finally, we look at the political and cultural considerations that may play a role. These assume even greater importance if you're operating outside your home territory. Like many aspects of business, bidding has become increasingly global. This creates both risks as well as opportunities. Some of the risks may not be so evident, especially if you're entering an unfamiliar market. We point out some of the pitfalls and bear traps we've encountered that can surprise the unwary.

In the end, it all comes back to preparation!

Key themes in Part I

➡ Understand the bidding supply chain[s] which you're involved in, and where you fit in this picture.

➡ Load the dice in your favour by having a clear bidding strategy which aligns with your organisation's overall strategy, and plays to its strengths.

➡ Do not settle for the status quo: set and monitor performance improvement targets.

➡ Focus is essential: you frequently achieve more by doing less.

➡ Be ruthless about not wasting time and resources bidding for work you have little or no chance of winning.

➡ Integrate Sales and Marketing into your bidding planning.

➡ If expanding outside your home market, undertake thorough preparation.

➡ Map the requirements of the project against the resources of the business, so you don't end up saddled with the winner's curse!

A Bird's Eye View: the Bidding Supply Chain

MANY BID WRITERS, even career professionals, only ever get to see a small part of the whole picture. By virtue of our role working across many sectors and advising numerous businesses at different stages of the bidding supply chain, we've been privileged to get a bird's eye view of that totality.

In the book's Preface we referred to the number of bids and people involved in constructing and operating a new school building, a typical example of a routine project put out to tender every week. We estimated that up to 150 separate bids would be submitted and up to 450 people could be involved, to get to the point where a new Academy opens its doors and actually starts teaching classes. This example is taken from the UK, but could apply anywhere where bidding for contracts is common practice.

In any significant project, it's the main contractors who make the headlines. But they are just the tip of the iceberg. It's only when we get beneath the surface of our example that we get the full picture of who is involved.

First, the actual construction of the new school building. This involves the following:

A Pre-Qualification Questionnaire (PQQ) for the main contract. This will attract multiple applications from all the major contractors who work nationwide and all the local contractors, including those who specialise in educational buildings. So you can easily end up with, say, 30 plus companies having to complete a detailed application to get to the next stage. That implies at least 30 bid teams at work. The purpose of this questionnaire is for the government client to end up with a shortlist of approximately six companies, which are then invited to submit bids for the main contract.

Next, bid teams from the six selected companies will complete a very detailed tender, and a winner is chosen: the Main Contractor.

The Main Contractor will have divided all the work into specialist *packages*. These are typically sent to three to six subcontractors to bid for and, again, these companies have to fill in a tender for the works, covering the sort of questions that demonstrate to the Main Contractor that they are capable of carrying out the work. This is typically a Method Statement, accompanied by Risk Assessments. Providing the information required is often a problem for a small subcontractor, as the person running the firm has the day job to see to, so some big companies will assist smaller businesses to guide them on to their Approved Supplier lists.

The Main Contractor will typically put the work out as:

➼ The Architectural Design Package

➼ The Structural Engineering Design Package

➼ The Ground Works

➼ The Building Works

➼ The Steel Package

➼ The Roofing Package

➼ The Mechanical and Electrical Package

➼ The Fitting-Out Works

➡ The Joinery Package

➡ The Windows Package

➡ The Security Package

➡ The Building Maintenance Package

➡ The Landscape Maintenance Package

➡ Facilities Maintenance

➡ Cleaning

➡ Sports Facilities

Experience suggests that, to create a competitive market in every case, each package goes to four subcontractors, who all have to bid for the work. That adds up to another 64 bids that all need writing, in addition to the 36 that have already been submitted. So it would not be unreasonable to expect that for *one* building to be built, 100 bid writers/ bid writing teams will have to submit bids with, on average, three people contributing written elements to each bid.

That amounts to 64 applications to get to a shortlister interview of, say, three organisations, after which each contract is awarded. But it doesn't end there. We have only got to the point where we have an empty school building! The story continues…

Second, operating the building. If the building is then to be run as an Academy [by a private company], the tendering starts again. More pre-qualification documents are completed. These are very detailed, as we know from our own experience – and then those shortlisted are invited to complete an equally detailed tender. To give you but one example, we have had a team of five people working with their counterpart team of ten plus, all focused on *one* Academy bid.

Even the bus companies are invited to tender, to take children to the school. Then there are grant funding applications. There is often a detailed application to Sport England that needs to be applied for, and so on. In conclusion, it would be a fair assumption that *as many as 450 people* will have contributed written elements in submitting bids before the one building opens for business. It's a big, drawn-out undertaking, that could last two years or even longer. The process is shown in Table 2.

Table 2: Bidding for a new school building

Stage	No. of bids	Bidding Teams	People involved at, say, three per bid
PQQ for main contract	30	30	90
Shortlist of bids for main contract: detailed bids	6	6	18
Total	**36**	**36**	**Minimum 90; Maximum 108**

Outcome: contract awarded to main contractor.

Subcontract packages	16 x 4 = 64	64	192

Outcome: contracts awarded: empty school building.

PQQ to run Academy	10	10	30
Shortlisted contracts to run Academy	3 shortlisted	3	30–39
Subcontractors to supply bid-for services [packages]	30	30	90
Total	**40–50**	**43**	**Minimum 150; Maximum 159**

[Best estimates of bids submitted. The assumptions underlying these calculations are laid out in Appendix 1.1.]

Outcome: school up and running.

Beating the Odds

READERS OF THIS book could be involved at any stage of this complex food chain, or one like it. Our experience is that, across sectors, bid success rates average around 12.5%. In view of the sheer numbers of organisations and bidding teams engaged in the bidding process, you might think that a win rate of one-in-seven is not a bad batting average. We'd draw your attention to the following points, however:

- The odds of winning differ dramatically *depending on the number of rival bids at each stage*. This applies to all bids which could be described as complex or protracted. Even if you discount all other factors affecting success, and assume all bids have an equal chance at the start, the odds of succeeding against 29 other organisations at the PQQ stage [1 out of 30] are far worse than the odds of succeeding against five other shortlisters [1 out of 6]. It makes sense, therefore, to avoid any errors that impair your chances early on. In Part II, we take you through the commonest mistakes that many bidders make which prevent them getting to the shortlist. With forethought and planning, all are easily avoided, **but too many organisations make them repeatedly**.

- An average is just that. Over a broad population some will do better, others worse. The bigger the population, the more extreme that divergence is likely to be.

➤ Our belief, founded on many years of experience, is that not only are all bids *not* created equal, but that you can load the dice *in your favour*. Maximising your chances of winning is what this book is all about. And the best place to start is by creating a strategy.

Creating a Bid Writing Strategy

IN THE ANNUAL planning round, businesses that have reached a certain level of size and maturity work on their strategy. At the top level there'll be a strategy for the company and supporting this there are typically strategies for Marketing, Sales, Finance, Logistics and so forth. These will detail the objectives of the various functions and spell out the activities and initiatives that support these. In a successful business that knows where it's going all the parts will fit together and someone reading the plan will quickly grasp what this business is all about and where it's heading. The plan doesn't have to be voluminous: sometimes brevity is a virtue that means the plan is more likely to serve as a road map, rather than sit on the shelf, unread.

Even with all this business planning and strategy, in our experience rarely will there be a bid writing strategy. Maybe that's not so important in companies that derive little of their business from winning tenders. What has surprised us, and continues to surprise us, is how few companies that earn a significant amount of their revenues through bidding have anything remotely resembling a strategy for this. Instead many adopt the bucket-of-mud approach, explained in the box overleaf.

The bucket-of-mud approach

It works like this:

1. Take a bucket.

2. Fill it with mud.

3. Fling it against a wall.

4. See how much sticks.

5. If not enough sticks, find a bigger bucket and repeat the process.

Translated into bid writing, this equates to:

1. Start the year with a blank page.

2. Bid at random for projects that come up broadly in our sector.

3. Increasingly panic as we fail to secure enough business.

4. Bid for anything and everything.

5. Repeat until company bid writers die or quit.

The bucket-of-mud strategy will definitely *not* load the dice in your favour. A proper strategy for bid writing, on the other hand, will get you off to the right start.

A fair question, then, to ask is what do we mean by a bid writing strategy? Pretty much the first question you should ask yourself is: what are you *really* good at? This general question can be usefully broken down into a number of supplementary questions:

➻ In your industry, what are you renowned for?

➻ If a customer recommends you to others, on what basis do they make a referral? Is it, for example, your quality of customer service? Product excellence? Delivering on time and to budget? An innovative approach to solving tricky problems? A unique set of skills and competences? Excellence in a particular specialism? Solutions that are clearly tailored to the needs of the individual client? [You can no doubt add to the list.]

➻ Where and how can you demonstrate this strength or strengths?

These questions, as you can see, are straightforward yet go to the heart of what the business is about. The clearer the organisation is in its responses, the easier it is to set both a top-level strategy and a complementary strategy for writing bids. **A bid writing strategy that plays to an organisation's strengths is more likely to deliver greater profitability, reduced costs and less employee stress:**

➻ *Greater profitability* because the organisation is focused on what it does best.

➻ *Reduced costs* because the organisation is not wasting time and resources bidding for projects it has little or no prospect of winning.

➻ *Less employee stress* because there is a defined plan to work to and realistic targets in the short and medium term [as set out below].

Conversely, where there is effectively **no** bid writing strategy in an organisation, what we frequently see is a failure to control costs, a silo mentality, and the diffusion and dilution of resources:

➻ *A failure to control costs* because in the absence of a strategy the business is driven by events. Reacting at short notice invariably costs you money.

➻ *A silo mentality* because bid writers are left isolated without organisational support and are told to "just get on with it".

➻ *Diffusion and dilution of resources* as the organisation lurches from one short-term panic to another.

Linking Your Strategy to the Sales and Marketing Functions

ARE WE EXAGGERATING to make a point? To some extent, yes. Not every organisation that lacks a bid writing strategy conforms to this pattern. But the point is an important one. If you don't know where you're going, it's a matter of luck whether you end up in the place you want to get to. It follows that if your bid writing activity is not aligned with your Sales and Marketing strategies, it's a recipe for internal dissent and confusion, and the chances of meeting the organisation's goals are that much more unlikely. We see this at its most extreme when companies are getting close to the end of their financial year and falling well short of their targets. Desperation sets in and people work around the clock, bidding for anything and everything. The reality is that you seldom regain that lost ground.

Before we go further, a word about Sales and Marketing. In this book we lump these two terms together. We do so because what counts as Sales and what counts as Marketing varies enormously from one business to another. In organisations which sell business-to-business, the received wisdom is that Sales is essentially a transactional activity, working to short-term horizons and measured by short-term results, whereas Marketing is supposedly a strategic and long-term activity. The one function complements the other.

In practice it seems that many businesses either haven't read the textbooks or, if they have, they haven't taken much notice. We've worked with businesses where Sales has dominated, and Marketing has consisted of little more than producing brochures and overseeing websites, and with businesses where Marketing has been top dog and the Sales function has been reduced to order-taking. In many cases it seems that the way the cake is cut is the product chiefly of the organisation's culture, tempered by the practices of the market sector(s) it operates in.

From the bid writing perspective it matters less how these functions are structured, and more how they collectively inform the bid writing strategy. Whatever their respective remits, Sales and Marketing need to deliver the following:

1. **Broad market intelligence**: A wide view of the market, how it is developing, the major factors which are impacting on it [such as government policy, legislative changes and so forth] and how it is likely to change over the planning period.

2. **Narrow market intelligence**: Specific developments in the sectors of the market where the organisation operates.

3. **Likely bidding opportunities** arising out of 1 and 2.

This is the essential groundwork and it is not difficult to do. The best way to integrate the bid writing function is to ensure that the bid writing team is included in the analysis, discussion and circulation list of all those involved in the bidding process, both inside the organisation and external to it, right from the outset. This achieves two things:

1. It enables the bid writing team to contribute their knowledge and insights to the shaping of the strategy, to make it realistic and coherent.

2. The team that will ultimately deliver the sales by writing the bids that win business buys into the strategy, because they have had a hand in formulating it.

Building the Plan and Creating Improvement Objectives

THE MOST EFFECTIVE planning processes we have seen are those that work *both* top down *and* bottom up. So far the process we have been describing is really top down. It needs to be balanced by working the plan from the bottom up. In planning generally, that implies breaking the plan down into manageable portions, usually by three-monthly quarters. It's exactly the same with bid writing.

Let's go back to the example company we featured in the Preface, under the section '**Competing to Win**'. It's a fairly typical business earning its living through bidding for and delivering projects, with a typical batting average. In the current year, the business has a bid success rate which is the same as the average bid success rate of its industry as a whole – 12.5%. The average value of a project won is 2m – you choose the currency. As things currently stand, to win a targeted ten projects and hit revenue targets, our business needs to bid for 88 projects.

Senior management has been reviewing the company's performance and concluded that it could up its bid writing game for this coming year. The message has been passed down the line. The Marketing team has taken stock of the business environment and thinks conditions are favourable: there's plenty of activity and forecasters are predicting steady growth. The Sales department has looked at media coverage of projects announced for the sector, sounded out key contacts and can identify a strong pipeline of tenders coming down the track. At a meeting of Sales, Marketing and the Bid Writing team it's agreed that **next** year they'll plan to bid for fewer projects, increase their success rate and secure more business.

Easy perhaps on paper, but how is it going to happen? You can't, as they say, eat an elephant all at once. You need to break a big, ambitious goal into manageable tasks. The Bid Writing team therefore breaks the 12-month plan into four quarters.

Our team has quite sensibly concluded that it can't achieve a miraculous improvement in success rates overnight, but it can build momentum through the year, which will produce the required improvement over the planning period. In Q1 they will continue with business as usual, while identifying those bids they have the best chance of winning in the following three quarters. The historic poor performance in Q4 is the result of team exhaustion in the previous quarters, resulting from the lack of any bidding strategy and the desperate, random bidding activities that have ensued. This time around, a planned approach should enable the team to improve its performance significantly. The impact is shown on the page opposite.

Case study exhibit A: The impact of a bidding strategy

Historical practice

Current Financial Year	Bids Submitted			Key Observations/ Actions
	No. of Bids	% Success Rate	No. Project Wins	Bid team of 6
Q1	10	20%	2	Bid team bidding for too many projects with little or no focus
Q2	10	30%	3	Improvement through effort
Q3	40	10%	4	Bid team behind target, over-bidding and failing
Q4	20	5%	1	Bid team burned out and failing, with knock-on effect for others, e.g. estimators
Full Year Figures	80	12.5%	10	
Currency £ sterling				
Average Bid Cost		£20,000		
Total Bidding Cost		£1.60m		
Average Project Size won		£2.00m		

Current Financial Year	Bids Submitted	Key Observations/ Actions
Total Project Value Won within the Year	£20.00m	
Overall Net profit @ 4% margin	£0.80m	
Net Bidding Cost or Surplus	− £0.80m	£0.8m − £1.6m

As you can see, in the current year the business spends 8% of its secured project income on bidding. At an overall net margin of 4%, that equals a net bidding cost to the business of £800,000. Not a good situation, but typical of the position many businesses find themselves in.

Future practice

Next Financial Year	Bids Submitted			Key Observations/ Actions
	No. of Bids	% Success Rate	No. Project Wins	
Q1	10	20%	2	Bid steadily, but focus on winnable bids for Qs 2 through 4
Q2	14	35%	4	Improve Success Rate and Project Wins through focus
Q3	10	40%	4	Improve Success Rate and Project Wins through focus

Next Financial Year	Bids Submitted			Key Observations/ Actions
	No. of Bids	% Success Rate	No. Project Wins	Bid team of 5
Q4	10	40%	4	Reduce team burnout through forward planning & steady state activity
Full Year Figures	**44**	**32%**	**14**	
Currency £ sterling				
Average Bid Cost	£30,000			£10,000 Increase per Bid
Total Bidding Cost	£1.32m			£480,000 Reduction
Average Project Size won	£2.50m			£0.50m Project Size Increase
Total Project Value Won within the Year	£35.00m			£13.0m Value Increase
Overall Net profit @ 6% margin	£2.10m			£1.3m Revenue Increase
Net Bidding Cost or Surplus	£0.78m			£1.58m Turnaround over previous year

A fundamental rethink of the organisation's bidding strategy has produced a significant turnaround. The value of projects won has increased by over 50%, the net margin has increased from 4% to 6%, and bidding activity has been transformed from a cost to an investment that generates a measurable return. At £1.32m, the money spent on bidding has actually fallen by nearly £300,000 and yet the business has actually bid for fewer projects and achieved a revenue increase of £1.3m.

How can this be possible?

Essentially the organisation has ceased to "spray and pray" and has been much more selective over the opportunities it has chosen to bid for [44 as opposed to 80 the year before]. A higher investment in bids it is more likely to win produces much greater average value per bid submitted, and enables Sales and Marketing to play to their strengths. Focus means better market intelligence. Specifically, the business has:

➻ Highlighted bids with a greater Quality[3] scoring element, which means better margins.

➻ Reduced the number of submitted bids by nearly half, allowing more time for thinking and planning and leading to less stress all round.

➻ Changed its understanding of bidding to be an investment, rather than a cost.

➻ Focused on margin.

As a result, the business is more sustainable and has created the foundation for further improvements to its bidding strategy in future years.

Key benefits of a proper bidding strategy:

➻ Refocus direction and thus effort.

➻ Sales and Marketing play to their strengths.

---

3   Quality is defined as an objective measure of the answers to the questions posed in the tender. Where the tender makes this explicit, it is easier for a bidder to produce answers that fully satisfy the questions in the eyes of the scorer. In tenders of this type, quality is valued highly and there is less likely to be pressure on price and thus an opportunity for the bidder to build better margin into their submission.

- Higher investment per bid delivers much greater average value per bid submitted and won.
- Being selective over opportunities increases the average size of each project bid for.
- Improved market intelligence.

Increasing the effort and investment in winning each opportunity leads to:

- Highlighting bids with a greater Quality scoring element, which means better margins.
- Fewer bids undertaken leads to more time for thinking and planning, which means less stress.
- Bidding seen as an investment, not just a cost of doing business.
- Increasing the margin from 4% to 6% through focus on profitable bids that you can win by emphasis on quality.
- Overall, reduction in bid costs produces a net surplus of £0.78m, an impressive turnaround of £1.58m!

These actions deliver:

- Reduced costs of bidding.
- Increase in revenue.
- A growing and sustainable business.
- An opportunity to reassess the future bidding strategy to make further improvements over the next financial year.
- Less stress on operations team by having fewer bigger jobs.

Hard Benefits and Soft Benefits of a Bid Writing Strategy

THE EXAMPLE THAT we have shown in the case study is based on our many years of working on bid submissions. We have seen two types of value which a well thought-through, informed bid writing strategy delivers.

1. Hard benefits

Hard benefits are those to which we can confidently attach numbers. In the case study, we can see that **focus** delivers more bang for your buck. By opting to bid for fewer, larger bids, the business gets a return on its investment in bid writing, instead of incurring a cost: a surplus of £0.78m instead of a cost of £0.8m. That's a turnaround of £1.58m, that goes straight to the bottom line.

It's true that each bid now costs more to submit, but the crucial point is that the *added value of each bid submitted* is greater, both because the success rate has more than doubled and the average value of each project won is £0.5m higher.

Why? Because the team has had time to think and plan! The organisation can also operate with a reduced number of bid writers, five instead of six[4], because they are writing fewer bids that they are more confident of winning – and that reduces the fixed overheads of the business.

2. Soft benefits

Soft benefits are the positive impacts that are more difficult to quantify, but equally beneficial. If the team is under less pressure there will be less staff burnout and churn, which reduces sick days and recruitment costs. When the success rate goes up, so does morale. Your people are working for a winner, and that sense of winning spreads through the organisation. There is a wider impact beyond the immediate Bidding, Sales and Marketing teams. For instance, estimators who are not under constant pressure because they are deluged with jobs are less prone to make mistakes.

A planned approach should also deliver two other important benefits. First, the Bid Writing team can better estimate the resources they need to achieve each quarter's targets – chiefly people and money – and specifically whether those resources exist in-house or need to be supplemented with outside help. Second, the team can begin to identify which tenders they should definitely *not* be bidding for – which brings us neatly on to the next topic.

---

4   Displaced bid writers need have no fear: the demand for bid writers is stronger than ever, and is set to go even higher!

To Bid or not to Bid?

The bids you don't want to win – five early warning signs:

1. Unacceptably high financial and/or managerial risk.

2. No good reason to bid: for example, "It's the next on the list…", or "The Chairman lives nearby."

3. High profile, but high risk, little reward and high impact of failure. Don't make headline news for the wrong reasons!

4. Can you actually resource the work if you win it?

5. Is it really your kind of work?

IN THE INTRODUCTION we expressed some scepticism about management gurus, magic bullets and prescriptions for business success. It's perhaps time to moderate this a little. Not all are tarred with the same brush. One thinker we consistently admire is Michael Porter of Harvard Business School, who has contributed much insight over a long career as a business analyst and commentator. One of those most striking insights relates to strategy and to choice: that choosing *what not to do* is equally as important, if not more important, than *what you choose to do*. Even the biggest corporation cannot fight on every front, all the time, and if you have 25 declared priorities effectively you have zero priorities.

The rubber really hits the road when we put our bid writing strategy under the microscope and start examining the pros and cons of going for a particular bid. Success in business is often about avoiding costly mistakes. Cut your losses early and, even better, don't get into deep water at the outset. Below we have highlighted five early warning signs that spell likely trouble ahead.

1. Unacceptably high financial and/or managerial risk

Experienced businesspeople understand the dangers of having too much business with any one customer. If the customer gets into trouble, or the relationship changes in a significant way, your own business can be put at risk. The same logic applies to bidding. If the size of the bid is out of your league, a win will stretch your resources to the limit and possibly to breaking point. The costs of servicing the contract will escalate, consuming your cash, and while your attention is focused on servicing this particular project others will suffer.

There's also managerial risk. Some bidders will see the solution to this as forming in effect a consortium, through planning to subcontract a significant portion of the project to others. The thinking is that this will reduce the risk, by spreading it. Frequently the opposite occurs. The risks of delivering on time, to specification and budget are compounded because you are relying on others to deliver your contractual commitments. Fine if you have reliable partners whom you can depend on, but disastrous if they let you down, and you consume even more time and expense managing your subcontractors and making good their deficiencies. In the worst case it spirals into litigation: nice work for the lawyers, but very bad news for you.

2. No good reason to bid

These are the bids driven by unthinking internal process, whim or desperation. There is no good strategic reason to bid for the work – in fact winning this is likely to be a continuing headache and runs counter to the direction of the business's overall strategy. Don't go there!

3. High profile, but high risk, little reward and high impact of failure

These are the seductive tenders, the boxes of chocolates that are hard to resist but will lead to chronic indigestion if you overindulge. A typical example is the iconic project – a landmark building perhaps – which senior management believes will put the company permanently on the map. Maybe. There is, however, a fine line between an iconic project and a vanity project that carries an unusually high level of reputational risk, makes little or no money and, if it goes wrong, does indeed put you in the headlines, for all the wrong reasons.

4. Can you actually resource the work if you win it?

This is the kind of bid we refer to as the *winner's curse*. We can best describe this as like acquiring the car of your dreams only to find that it breaks down frequently, the fuel consumption is twice what you expected and the running costs are off the scale. It doesn't take long for what should have been one of the highlights of a lifetime to turn into a nightmare. So it is with the winner's curse. Once you've won, the euphoria rapidly wears off as reality sets in. If you find internal resources can't cope, the usual recourse is to turn to subcontractors to help out – and that opens the whole potential can of worms that we've just described above.

5. Is it really your kind of work?

And this last point brings us back to something we can't stress highly enough: the value of focus. If you're a big, multi-disciplinary, multi-divisional business, *your kind of work* might cover a very broad range of viable projects. But most businesses don't fit that description, and if yours does not, don't kid yourself. There's a lot of truth in the adage of *horses for courses*.

The Bid/No Bid tool

The only sure way to avoid bidding for and winning projects you live to regret is through a structured and disciplined process, that involves the key internal stakeholders. In Appendix 1.2 we've reproduced our full template that provides the necessary rigour when evaluating an invitation to tender [ITT]. Below is a worked example that shows how a cut-down version of this methodology can be applied in real bidding situations, where potential opportunities are screened in or out right from the start.

The Bid/No Bid form: worked examples

Initial screening of tenders: the business in question has capacity to manage contracts with a value between £10,000 and £200,000. Bidder profile:

➸ SME company – Providing marketing support and based in East Midlands of England.

➸ Industry Sector – Marketing and Advertising.

➸ Able to use and demonstrate innovations such as internet-based marketing campaigns and physical stands (with 3D screens) within public areas.

Sample – Bid No Bid Form

QUALIFICATION QUESTIONS:

	Score	Weighting	Total	Comments
Q1. Is the contract of the correct value (£200,000 Max, £10,000 Min)?				
Yes/No		PASS/FAIL		Score 1 for Yes and score 0 for 'No'
Q2. Can we resource the Operational aspects?				
Yes/No		PASS/FAIL		Score 1 for Yes and score 0 for 'No'

NOTE: IF WE SCORE A 'FAIL' ON QUESTION 1 OR 2 THEN WE DO NOT BID.

QUALITY QUESTIONS:

	Score	Weighting	Total	Comments
Q3. Do we have the relevant experience to deliver this project?				
Yes/No		30%	0.00	Score up to 10 for 'Yes' and up to 4 for 'No'

	Score	Weighting	Total	Comments
Q4. Does Price outweigh Quality?				
Yes/No		20%	0.00	Score 2 for 'Yes' and up to 10 for 'No'
Q5. Is the location of the contract within a suitable distance?				
Yes/No		20%	0.00	Score up to 10 for 'Yes' and 4 for 'No'
Q6. Is the incumbent underperforming on the contract?				
Yes/No		10%	0.00	Score 10 for 'Yes' and 4 for 'No'
Q7. Do we have suitable USPs that we can bring to this project?				
Yes/No		20%	0.00	Score up to 10 for 'Yes' and up to 2 for 'No'
		100%	0.00	
	Score		0	

Score values	Suggested outcome
Above 90%	Key Target
81%–90%	Definite Bid
70%–81%	Proceed but check priorities
60%–69%	Check details & Refer to Management
55%–60%	No Bid/Refer to Management
Below 55%	Check details & No Bid

Example A: Arriving at a No Bid decision for a tender

➤ Medium-sized project.

➤ Contract value £40,000 – for an online marketing campaign.

➤ Can be resourced, plus the business has the experience to deliver this project.

➤ Price outweighs quality – the tender has specified that price considerations are weighted 70%, quality considerations 30%.

➤ Not within a suitable distance – i.e. based in Glasgow, Scotland.

➤ We do not know how the incumbent is performing.

➤ There is very little innovation that we feel we can introduce to this. Much of what we already offer is included within the project specification.

The example below produces a score of 46, which means a definite No Bid.

Example A – Bid No Bid Form – No Bid Scenario

QUALIFICATION QUESTIONS:

	Score	Weighting	Total	Comments
Q1. Is the contract of the correct value (£200,000 Max, £10,000 Min)?				
Yes/No	1	PASS/FAIL	PASS	Score 1 for Yes and score 0 for 'No'
Q2. Can we resource the Operational aspects?				
Yes/No	1	PASS/FAIL	PASS	Score 1 for Yes and score 0 for 'No'

NOTE: IF WE SCORE A 'FAIL' ON QUESTION 1 OR 2 THEN WE DO NOT BID.

QUALITY QUESTIONS:

	Score	Weighting	Total	Comments
Q3. Do we have the relevant experience to deliver this project?				
Yes/No	9	30%	2.70	Score up to 10 for 'Yes' and up to 4 for 'No'

	Score	Weighting	Total	Comments
Q4. Does Price outweigh Quality?				
Yes/No	2	20%	0.40	Score 2 for 'Yes' and up to 10 for 'No'
Q5. Is the location of the contract within a suitable distance?				
Yes/No	3	20%	0.60	Score up to 10 for 'Yes' and 4 for 'No'
Q6. Is the incumbent underperforming on the contract?				
Yes/No	5	10%	0.50	Score 10 for 'Yes' and 4 for 'No'
Q7. Do we have suitable USPs that we can bring to this project?				
Yes/No	2	20%	0.40	Score up to 10 for 'Yes' and up to 2 for 'No'
		100%	4.60	
	Score		46	

Example B: Arriving at a decision to Bid

➤ Larger-sized project.

➤ Contract value £100,000 – looking for a multi-faceted marketing campaign around a new product range (both internet and physical) that matches our profile.

➤ Can be resourced, plus we have the experience to deliver this project.

➤ Even split on quality-price – price 50%, quality 50%.

➤ Based in Northampton – much closer.

➤ We know there are problems with the client's current marketing provider.

➤ We can provide the physical marketing stands at a slightly cheaper price than competitors can.

The example below produces a score of 82, which means a definite Bid.

Example B – Bid No Bid Form – Definite Bid Scenario

QUALIFICATION QUESTIONS:

	Score	Weighting	Total	Comments
Q1. Is the contract of the correct value (£200,000 Max, £10,000 Min)?				
Yes/No	1	PASS/FAIL	PASS	Score 1 for Yes and score 0 for 'No'
Q2. Can we resource the Operational aspects?				
Yes/No	1	PASS/FAIL	PASS	Score 1 for Yes and score 0 for 'No'

NOTE: IF WE SCORE A 'FAIL' ON QUESTION 1 OR 2 THEN WE DO NOT BID.

QUALITY QUESTIONS:

	Score	Weighting	Total	Comments
Q3. Do we have the relevant experience to deliver this project?				
Yes/No	9	30%	2.70	Score up to 10 for 'Yes' and up to 4 for 'No'

	Score	Weighting	Total	Comments
Q4. Does Price outweigh Quality?				
Yes/No	5	20%	1.00	Score 2 for 'Yes' and up to 10 for 'No'
Q5. Is the location of the contract within a suitable distance?				
Yes/No	9	20%	1.80	Score up to 10 for 'Yes' and 4 for 'No'
Q6. Is the incumbent underperforming on the contract?				
Yes/No	9	10%	0.90	Score 10 for 'Yes' and 4 for 'No'
Q7. Do we have suitable USPs that we can bring to this project?				
Yes/No	9	20%	1.80	Score up to 10 for 'Yes' and up to 2 for 'No'
		100%	8.20	
		Score	82	

This tool is in many ways a mirror-image of the methodology which tendering organisations employ to score the bids they receive. As far as possible it makes the decision an objective and structured one. The examples above show how use of the tool for initial screening prevents a business pursuing opportunities that might look superficially attractive, but are taking it in the wrong direction, wasting time, money and internal resources. This approach also avoids the opportunity cost of not focussing on bids that *are* a good fit with the organisation's strategy and capabilities.

The extended version of this tool shown in Appendix 1.2 is designed to achieve a number of purposes:

➼ *Clarity* over who does what. Too often we have seen what might have been a winning bid fail, purely because someone has dropped the baton. A thinks B was going to do X. B thinks A was going to do X. As a result no one does X, but without X the bid is bound to fail. It happens because people are fallible. A robust process, if followed closely, is less likely to fail.

➼ *Accountability and responsibility* follow from clarity. There's little or no room for hiding away, and less time wasted in pointing the finger and playing infantile corporate politics. There's a requirement to act as adults, playing to a common set of rules.

➼ *Reality check.* If everyone who is going to play a part in putting the bid together is enrolled in the process, then there is a collective understanding of the commitment required. The emphasis changes from speculation to delivery. A bid that is fundamentally unrealistic is flagged early on – and you stand less chance of being saddled with the winner's curse if you actually succeed!

➼ *Time-saving.* A document that spells out the process enables you to get the creation and submission of the bid off to a flying start. If you decide to proceed it will provide the basis of the agenda for the Kick-Start meeting which we describe in Part II.

You might wish to create a version of this template specific to your business and your needs as you see them. If you do so, ensure it achieves the same purposes as we've outlined above.

Preparing for Battle

L ET'S ASSUME THAT you've made the decision to bid. The project fits with the strategy of the business, it scores well on your internal evaluation template and your chances of success meet your threshold. But before you start, remember the *value of research*.

No bid takes place in a vacuum. There's a history and a context and you need to understand both. We've seen the value in the old military saying to the effect that time spent in reconnaissance is seldom wasted: an effective commander scouts the territory well in advance of engaging the troops. The commander grasps the terrain on which the battle will take place, and positions their forces to gain maximum advantage.

The intelligence you need to gather can be summarized in three key questions:

1. **What role does this project play in the wider scheme of things?** For example, in government procurement an ITT is usually part of a programme that will run over an extended period of time. This might be a plan for the regeneration of a city, or renewal of a transport network. It could well be a pet project championed by an influential individual, and could have been several years in the making. It could be the preserve of a number of groups who have lobbied for it and will be represented at interviews for shortlisted bidders. Understand the key factors at play and you'll have a sharper sense of what aspects of your submission should carry greater influence.

2. **What are the client's strategic aims?** Unless it's a one-off and standalone exercise, the project is likely to have key linkages and dependencies. These are longer term and often form part of a larger agenda, such as the creation of an enduring legacy. Anything connected to a major international sporting event would fall into this category. The hosting of an Olympic Games is well known as a classic case of winner's curse and many host cities have been left with an enduring legacy they wish they had never signed up to: crumbling stadia, enormous maintenance and debt servicing bills and an infrastructure that cannot be repurposed. The planning of London 2012, for example, went to huge lengths to learn from the misfortunes of its predecessor hosts. Sustainable re-usage and the regeneration of east London were major elements in the strategic thinking behind the city's bid, to create the right kind of legacy. Those bidders who grasped and reflected these concerns in their submissions will understandably have been viewed more favourably.

3. **How important is the project?** The answers to the questions already posed should give you a good sense of the relative importance of the project to the tendering organisation and to key individuals within that organisation. If it's a great success, who stands to benefit? If it fails in any major way, is this career-limiting? How much is at stake and, as a consequence, how risk-averse is the client likely to be? Take account of these factors, and your bid is more likely to succeed.

You do not need to spend weeks in research and produce reams of paper to address this. A precise summary of no more than two pages is enough to serve as a briefing paper that will actually be read by the bidding team, and will pay dividends as a refresher if you make the shortlist for interview.

Where West meets East

Fly into Beijing Capital International Airport and, as the plane descends to land, look out of the window. The first thing that will probably strike you is a vast, soaring, aerodynamic roof. Look closely and you'll see that it's formed in the shape of a dragon, the ancient symbol of China that permeates the country's myths, history and culture. Once you disembark and enter the terminal itself, you will see colours and designs that signal you've arrived in Asia's largest and most populous nation.

The airport was designed and constructed in four short years between 2003 and 2007, opening bang on schedule for the 2008 Beijing Olympics. The master planners behind this magnificent structure were Foster + Partners, the London-based multi-disciplinary architectural practice and creators of iconic structures across the globe. The thinking behind this project? Foster + Partners said: "Designed to be welcoming and uplifting, it is also a symbol of place, its soaring aerodynamic roof and dragon-like form celebrating the thrill and poetry of flight and evoking traditional Chinese colours and symbols."

Hardly surprising, then, that their bid was the winner in a fiercely competitive tendering process, and proof of the value of understanding the political and cultural factors at play.

Political and Cultural Considerations

THE PHRASE *GLOBALIZATION* is one of the most overused in modern business vocabulary. That doesn't detract from the fact that the value and volume of international trade have increased enormously in the last 20 years as tariff and non-tariff barriers have reduced and developing economies have grown rapidly.

Alongside that, we are now at a point where advanced economies need to renew their ageing infrastructures and emerging economies need to invest in creating theirs. Opportunities to bid for projects have never been so plentiful. Cross-border tendering offers great scope for ambitious businesses to spread their wings, especially those that operate in a limited home market.

At the same time, those opportunities contain their fair share of pitfalls and bear traps. Examples of companies that haven't done their homework properly are legion. Even the biggest corporations make elementary mistakes. If we just take the auto industry, GM came away with mud on their face when they launched the Nova model in Latin America without first checking the meaning of "no va" ["it doesn't go"] in Spanish and Portuguese. Rolls-Royce almost went to market with a model christened the Silver Mist before someone alerted them to the fact that in German "mist" translates as "dung". Trivial examples, you think? Not when millions of dollars, pounds and deutschmarks are at stake and your credibility is at risk.

Ease of doing business

In the book's Preface we presented a table based on data compiled by the IMF, ranking the expenditure on tendered contracts by national governments. Below we show the same table again, and add for comparison a ranking of countries by *ease of doing business*. A new market may look attractive because of its sheer size, but if there are obstacles in terms of operating locally perhaps it's not such a good proposition on balance.

The US is a case in point. The market is enormous and it has the advantage – if you're an anglophone business – of being English-speaking. It's ranked number one in terms of bid value. Looked at from the outside, at a superficial glance this makes it very enticing and a natural first point of entry for ambitious foreign firms looking to grow outside their domestic market. However, the United States is not just one market. While federal legislation covers the whole country, local legislation and regulation can differ widely from state to state, depending on industrial sector. Expanding into the US has brought grief to many well-known UK businesses, among them Tesco, Sainsbury and Marks & Spencer. A Cranfield School of Management survey of smaller UK firms that had set up in the US found that they typically underestimated the challenges posed by the sheer size of the country, its extremes of climate and the ferocity of local competition. It proved tougher than they expected. The US is also notoriously prone to litigation!

On the other hand, New Zealand is ranked world number one in terms of ease of doing business, and Singapore number two, although neither makes it into the top 19 in annual value of government procurement. They might be small markets, but their governments have made them attractive places to do business.

Table 3: World rankings by bid value versus world rankings by ease of doing business

Ranking by Bid Value			Ranking by Ease of Doing Business	
Rank	Country	US$ bn	Rank	Country
1	USA	19,377.2	1	New Zealand
2	EU [26 countries, excluding UK and Ireland]	14,360.1	2	Singapore
3	China [excluding Hong Kong]	12,362.0	3	Denmark
4	Japan	5,106.0	4	Hong Kong
5	UK and Ireland	2,609.9	5	South Korea
6	India	2,458.0	6	Norway
7	Canada	1,672.3	7	UK
8	Russia	1,442.0	8	USA
9	Australia	1,344.0	9	Sweden
10	Turkey	770.0	10	Macedonia
11	Saudi Arabia	689.0		
12	Switzerland	684.0		
13	Arab Emirates [excluding Qatar and Kuwait]	408.0		
14	Norway	393.0		
15	Hong Kong	326.0		
16	New Zealand	193.0		
17	Qatar	171.0		
18	Kuwait	125.0		
19	Iceland	21.4		

Source: The World Bank (www.data.worldbank.org/indicator/IC.BUS.EASE.XQ).

A high ranking for ease of doing business means the regulatory environment is more conducive to the starting and operation of a local firm. Of course not every foreign firm that bids for work outside its home territory will incorporate a local subsidiary, but this measure is a good proxy for how easy in general it is to operate in the markets concerned.

The measure is a composite of the following factors:

➻ Starting a business

➻ Registering property

➻ Getting credit

➻ Protecting minority investors

➻ Dealing with construction permits

➻ Trading across borders

➻ Paying taxes

➻ Getting electricity

➻ Resolving insolvency

➻ Enforcing contracts

In the first five of these categories, New Zealand was ranked top out of 190 countries reviewed.

Key questions to ask yourself

If you're considering expanding for the first time outside your home territory, research is vital. Here are some key questions that we think are worth addressing:

Which of these factors is important in your sector?

The metrics used in the World Bank survey will vary in significance by sector and so will vary in their importance for you, subject to the sector you operate in. For example, if the bid is for an infrastructure project the ease or difficulty with which construction permits are processed has a major impact on the smooth running of the project. If you can foresee that winning the tender means you will have to enter multiple contractual agreements, the ability to enforce those contracts in the event of dispute is going to be vital. Will you be able to repatriate your profits if you want to? Are there others in your sector that have done business in that jurisdiction who you can talk to about the helpfulness or otherwise of local banks to provide credit if needed? Take this opportunity to ask if there any other aspects of doing business in the territory concerned that, based on their experience, you should take account of.

Are there provisions for assistance in the tender?

Some, perhaps all, of the potential issues that come from doing business in a foreign country may be covered by assurances or statements of intent provided in the tender documentation. If so, good. After all, if the client is a national government or one of its agencies, it is in their interest to ensure the project runs smoothly. But – and there's nearly always a but – you need to be clear early on about what is under the client's direct control and what is not. As a general rule, the higher the issuing authority, the greater the clout. Thus if the project is being driven by a senior figure such as a government minister, you can expect your path to be eased if any hiccups arise. On the other hand, if it's under the control of someone more junior, you don't want to find that key members of your staff can't start work because their entry visas or temporary resident permits have been stalled in the system.

Is there a professional network to support you?

In your home market you already have the professional network of lawyers, banks and accountants to provide the support you need to operate as a business. If you've been in business a while, you almost certainly take this for granted. Like many things in life, you only really understand the value when it's no longer there. When you enter a new market, you have to recreate your network more or less from scratch. Often the professionals you are already using have corresponding relationships or informal links to their counterparts in other countries. That will be true of banks and if you are working with reasonably-sized lawyers and accountants they are more than likely to have connections that are useful. If you are using one-man bands as your professional advisers, you may well question whether these are the right people to support the business you aspire to be. Start the conversations early and you'll be better prepared for whatever lies ahead.

As each bid is unique it's impossible to provide guidance for every eventuality. In our experience of businesses that operate internationally, while you can't eliminate the business risks imposed by local regulation, advance planning can certainly reduce these to an acceptable level.

Classic political and cultural bear traps

There is a whole specialist management literature on the subject of cultural differences and we do not intend to reproduce that here. But in bid writing in particular we've seen people stumble unwittingly into bear traps which, with a little forethought, can be easily avoided. It's worth looking at some of these bear traps briefly here.

Check the political agenda

A consortium we know of bid for a project funded by the European Union. On the surface their submission was a shoo-in. They could demonstrate that the combined expertise of the partners was a perfect fit for the requirements of the programme and the bid answered all the questions posed in the tender. There was an ideal match – or so the bidders thought.

They made the shortlist but were disappointed and surprised to find they weren't successful. Although it was a pan-European project, the bid was to be evaluated by an organisation based in a southern European country.

Like its neighbours, this country was suffering from [and continues to suffer from] unprecedentedly high levels of youth unemployment. For years public policy-makers have been grappling with this and it continues to be the first item on the political agenda. Our consortium's bid made no reference as to how their proposal addressed this issue, though it could credibly have done so. In the feedback, their attention was drawn to what the reviewers saw as a fundamental omission.

On a narrow view, it was a great bid and it met the criteria of the tender. But the political antennae had failed to register what was top of mind in those scoring the bids.

You say tomato, I say tomayto

English is undeniably the international language of business. Indeed, today there are more speakers of English as a second language than people for whom English is their native tongue. There are, however, many varieties of English, even among native speakers. British English is not quite the same as American English, which is not quite the same as Australian English, etc. Although there are efforts to standardise a form of international English, some divergence is inevitable. The divergence might be nuanced, but might have a critical bearing on the way in which a bid submission is drafted. If the tender is *not* in English and/or the bid submission cannot be in English, make sure you factor in the translation charges early on by getting ball-park estimates. These costs can be very considerable and could increase your overall bidding costs by 50% or even 100%. Do not fall into the trap of using a generalist for your submission: to do an accurate and credible job, you need a specialist technical translator.

Same language does not mean same culture

If you pepper your submission with references that are specific to the culture you live and work in, and mean absolutely nothing to the recipient – or even worse, simply confuse them – don't be surprised if you don't make the shortlist. Flagging up that you're importing a whole lot of cultural baggage into the project isn't going to give the client comfort and, even worse, may well arouse sensitivities that lie below the surface. Are there, for example, historical links between your country of domicile and theirs which could, if not carefully handled, inflame such sensitivities?

You don't even have to cross the border

Even within one country there can be significant regional cultural and political divergences. As regular travelers to the US we have become alert to the differences, for example, between the east and west coasts and the distinctiveness of the Midwest. And once you cross the Mason-Dixon line into the American South, the visitor from out of town needs to revisit their assumptions about the country they find themselves in.

Avoiding bear traps

The best way to steer clear of bear traps is to anticipate them. Here is a list of strategies we have found to be effective.

1. There's a lot of truth in the observation that all politics is local. If you're unfamiliar with the territory you're bidding in, build some resource into your background research. It may take little more than an internet search of the local and regional press to establish what's on the minds of influencers and policy-makers. Log it and remember it.

2. Better still, if time and budget allow, tap into the opinions of people on the ground. If you seriously believe that a new market presents a good long-term opportunity, then establish a permanent presence. You can start small and expand if your bet proves well founded. An office on the ground demonstrates intent and commitment. UK embassies usually have a person – the commercial attaché – whose main role is to brief British businesses entering overseas markets, and they are frequently a mine of useful information and guidance. The UK government regularly organises overseas trade missions that provide opportunities to scout new territories or strengthen existing ties.

3. Keep the language you use in the submission simple and straightforward. That way, there's less room for misunderstanding. This is a subject we return to in greater detail later in the book.

4. If you have someone in your organisation who is native-born to the home country of the tenderer, have them read through the final submission and note their comments. Often this is not possible, but at the very least seek to identify someone in your organisation who is not native-born to *your* home country and have them check the document. He or she will see it through a different pair of eyes, and may be more alert to cultural sensitivities as a result. Again, this is a topic we expand on in Part II.

Map and Match

DRAWING TOGETHER THE key points of the previous sections, we summarise these in the concept of *mapping*: that's to say, mapping the requirements of the projects you are bidding for against the resources of the business. If you follow the kind of rigorous process laid out in the Bid/No Bid template you'll know exactly what's required of all those involved. Through systematic and detailed planning you will have greater confidence in the ability of the organisation to deliver its commitments if you achieve your bid targets. For most organisations, what keeps people awake at night is the spectre of failing to meet the targets, i.e. underachieving. Planning by quarter allows the time and space to recover and regroup if you fall short.

However, overachievement can be just as much of an issue. Admittedly this is the kind of problem most businesses would prefer to have, but if you're unprepared for an overload you face issues of stress and declining margins as you hastily put together the resource base needed to deliver the work. A planned approach will help identify the contingencies you're likely to need if your bid success rate outperforms expectations, or enables you to rein back your bidding activity in the next quarter. Either way, **you** make the choices and **you're** in the driving seat.

Related to mapping is the notion of *matching*. The most consistently successful bidders we've worked with have a keen sense of what kinds of projects to focus on. When they assess a tender, they evaluate the fit between their skills and experience and the requirements of the tender.

This is not confined just to the project: they almost always have a sense at the outset of whether there's a good organisational fit. In simple terms, it's a case of "do we want to/could we work with these people?" In business you don't always have the luxury of choosing your customers in the way you'd choose your friends. But if the chemistry works, the chances of a successful outcome are generally better, especially if you have to negotiate bumps in the road ahead.

Takeaways from Part I

→ It might be a cliché, but failing to plan is by and large planning to fail. Throwing a bucket of mud at a wall is not a bidding strategy – but it's what an awful lot of businesses do. Just having a plan puts you ahead of the game.

→ A credible strategy is based on what your business is good at. Play to your strengths and you're more likely to succeed.

→ Breaking the plan down into quarters and setting clear, measurable goals gives the organisation focus, and everyone something to aim for. Set one improvement goal per quarter and stick to it. Challenge the status quo. If you don't, you're condemned to live with it.

→ Be clear about what you're *not* going to do and don't get drawn into mission creep. Limit your priorities. One of the most successful financiers of his generation is John McFarlane. Now Chairman of Aviva, he was headhunted some years ago to turn around ANZ Bank, the leading provider of financial services in the southern hemisphere. In a relatively short time, he transformed the bank's fortunes. Asked how he did it, he explained that it was crucial at any one time to have three, and only three, priorities. The priorities changed over the years, but their number stayed the same. More to the point, everyone in the bank also knew what they were.

→ Do your background research thoroughly. Make sure you know the broader agenda of the client organisation and how the project fits within it. Be alert to the political and cultural dimensions of the work you're bidding for.

➠ Above all, keep it simple. Once you decide to bid, get everyone on the same page right from the start, so there's a collective understanding of what's needed for you to be successful.

PART II

CREATION, REVIEW AND PREPARATION FOR SHORTLISTING

Introduction

Part I was concerned with ensuring you and your organisation are in the best possible shape so that you are match-fit for writing and submitting bids. Every successful competitor has a training regime that gets them ready to perform at their peak. "Be prepared" said Robert Baden-Powell, and the scouting movement he founded, with this motto as its watchword, has developed into one of the most successful youth organisations in the world.

In Part II, we enter the race. Following a cautionary tale, we start by identifying the commonest mistakes that handicap bid submissions, the *Not-so Magnificent Seven*, and explain how these can be avoided from the start and as you work through bids. Eliminating these mistakes as an integral part of your processes greatly improves your chances of success.

Then we come to one of the keys to successful bid writing: the Kick-Start meeting, which sets the tone for each submission and defines the bid process from the moment you decide to go for a tender. We outline the people who need to be present at that meeting, their roles and responsibilities, the agenda for that meeting and the processes that flow from it. We return to the case study of our fictional business and show how a Kick-Start meeting is implemented in practice, and what needs to happen subsequently.

A well-structured Kick-Start meeting sets you on the right track. We recommend you then have follow-up bid review and monitoring processes to ensure your submissions remain on track through the cycle.

Then we get into the nitty-gritty of writing bids that clients actually *want* to read. There are three golden rules that give every bid a winning edge: follow these, and you're virtually guaranteed a place in the shortlist. They will also smooth the path when you are called for the shortlister interview. We outline what makes a compelling case study with a list of dos and don'ts in support of your credentials, and show you how to unpack and answer complex questions.

We've noticed an increasing trend for organisations tendering big projects to insert an extra round of Best and Final Offers [BAFOs]. If you've not encountered these before we explain what's involved and how to prepare, and share a case study in how to do this successfully.

We return to the subject of preparation when it comes to shortlister meetings. There are numerous steps you can take in advance of an interview which will present your team in the best possible light. At the meeting itself you have an opportunity to take control, without appearing overbearing or monopolising the conversation. Equally there are common mistakes which many bid teams make, and we'll show you how to anticipate and avoid these.

Finally, in advance of awarding the contract some clients may request a site visit, either to meet you at your office or to inspect a project you have managed. We walk through the stages of what these visits entail and show you how to present your team and your business to best advantage.

Key themes in Part II

➻ Avoiding the seven elementary errors that derail many bids at the outset.

➻ Getting off to the best possible start with a well-structured Kick-Start meeting.

➻ Being crystal-clear about who is responsible for doing what.

➻ Defining the follow-up processes that ensure your submission stays on track throughout.

➻ Writing bids that clients *want* to read by following the three golden rules.

➻ What is involved in a Best and Final Offer (BAFO).

➻ How to prepare for a shortlister meeting.

➻ Taking control of interviews: dos and don'ts.

➻ How to manage site visits in a way that shows your organisation to best advantage.

Avoiding Common Mistakes

W<small>E OPEN</small> P<small>ART</small> II with a story. A while ago we were approached for guidance on writing a significant bid. It involved working for an organisation where the bidding business had bid for work before, and was unsuccessful. We started by asking to see the previous submission, to see what we could learn from it.

This business had a standard process for submitting bids. They always put the logo of the business they were bidding to win work from on their documentation. On every page. In this instance, the target business absolutely prohibited the unauthorised use of their company logo. This was stated clearly in the bid guidelines. Their brand is known all over the world and is incredibly precious to them. What the bidder had done was to download this image, manipulate it digitally and plaster it everywhere on their bid documentation, just as they always did; they had simply ignored the submission guidelines. Their bid therefore had zero chance of succeeding. It didn't matter how good a bid it was: one look and it will have gone straight in the waste bin. When we sat down and pointed this out following our review, the bidder had an OMG moment.

You might be thinking this is a one-off. You'd *never* do something like that. Really? In our experience it happens every day: companies bidding for work ignore the submission guidelines. The episode described above happened to an organisation that secures over 80% of its work through successful bidding. It's been in business for many years. Too often bidders either don't read the guidelines, or they don't take them seriously. And then they wonder why they haven't been successful.

In this case, we dug a bit deeper, to understand what was going wrong. The business's attitude to bidding had become tired and formulaic. Success and failure was simply a numbers game. If sales were down, they just threw additional mud at the wall and crossed their fingers that more was going to stick. The problem was that this attitude was deeply engrained: when a new recruit was inducted into the team, he or she was told that this was the way it was and just to follow the process. Thus the culture was perpetuated.

The supreme irony was that this business operated in the field of corporate training, helping organisations improve their performance.

The Not-so Magnificent Seven: the common mistakes that derail bids

At the outset:

1. Not reading and adhering to the guidelines.

2. Not answering the questions.

As you work through the bid:

3. Failing to allocate page allowance in proportion to the scoring criteria.

4. Unstructured answers.

5. Favouring style over substance.

6. No added value included.

7. No evidence to support added value.

In Part II we walk you through the tactics, strategies and processes you can employ to make sure that, once you've decided to bid, you don't shoot yourself unwittingly in the foot. Part II also highlights what you can do to make your bid stand out from the crowd, and how best to prepare yourself for the face-to-face interview when you make the shortlist.

Simply by avoiding common errors you hugely increase your chances of succeeding against the rest of the field and securing the projects you really want to win. We've identified seven common mistakes that derail bids. With a little forethought and planning they can be easily avoided.

1. Not reading and adhering to the guidelines

We've found a number of reasons why this happens. Sometimes the cause is as simple as too little time and too much to do. Occasionally the explanation lies with the failure of the tendering organisation to get its act together, creating unrealistic deadlines, but more often than not the root cause is the lack of a planned approach to bid writing, as we outlined in Part I. In-house staff simply don't have the capacity to prepare properly, but just dive straight in. This type of problem is intensified if the organisation is falling behind its revenue targets and desperation has taken hold.

A more serious problem is of the kind outlined in the case study we began with. The bidding organisation is an acknowledged leader in its field, and that track record of success can bring with it a mentality that crosses the thin line between confidence and hubris: "We're the obvious choice to deliver this project. The rules apply to everyone else." That might just be the case 1% of the time, but it certainly isn't 99% of the time. In a competitive tender, the emphasis is on being *competitive*. The same set of rules apply to everybody who's bidding. Why prejudice your chances at the outset?

2. Not answering the questions

Some bidders will go to almost any lengths to avoid answering the questions asked by the tender. On first or even subsequent reading you might not understand why the tender asks a particular question. You might even think the question is irrelevant to the project, or unreasonable. Your opportunity to probe the client organisation, to get a better understanding of the thinking behind the questions, will come through requesting clarification and in the shortlister meeting. But if you don't answer the questions, you're never going to be attending that meeting.

3. Failing to allocate page, word or character allowance in proportion to the scoring criteria

These days a tender will normally specify the weighting given to each component of the bid. Table 4 shows a typical example.

This is the view *from the client* of the way submitted bids are going to be scored, reflecting what matters to them, and this needs to be mirrored in your submission. Chances are that you've got a restricted word, page or character count and a limited space in which to give your answers. If the tender indicates that a particular section will be scored out of 20% of the total, don't devote 50% of the available word count to that section. Inevitably you'll have to compromise on what you can say elsewhere, needlessly creating an opportunity for your competitors to capitalise on what you've omitted to write.

Table 4: Example of weighting criteria

Selection Criteria – Weighting of shortlisting questions

Criterion	Subject area	Weighting as a percentage of the marks available for quality of submitted bids
1	Experience of providing construction and related services	25%
2	Efficiencies, saving and continued improvement	20%
3	Integrated Service Management Systems	10%
4	Business Continuity	5%
5	Supply Chain Management	20%
6	Sustainability	10%
7	Skills and development	10%
Total		100%

4. Unstructured answers

Questions in tenders can sometimes be asked in a dense, complicated or vague way, that needs to be unpacked. Later in this part, in the section **'Writing bids that clients want to read'**, we address this issue in more detail, explaining how to separate the component parts of this kind of question and provide clear responses which are easy for the evaluator to score. For now, we'll just draw your attention to the following observations:

➵ A tender document is often put together in a hurry, for all sorts of reasons. That doesn't *necessarily* make it unattractive for you to bid for, if it's succeeded in passing the kind of scrutiny that we've outlined in Part I. That haste can surface in convoluted questions which, given time to revise, the person writing the tender could have expressed in a simpler, clearer form. A lot of bidders see this as just another headache. Turn the issue around, and see it as an opportunity to shine against rival bidders. If you can unpack, simplify and provide structured answers that are straightforward to evaluate, you've made someone's life significantly easier.

➻ The author of the tender may be relatively new to the job and inexperienced. It is often the case that he or she has never been in your shoes, responding to an ITT. Client organisations vary enormously in their induction and training practices when it comes to putting out tender documents. One former oil company executive we know well was so concerned after reviewing the disparity across issuing tenders inside his business that he designed and led a series of in-house training programmes to address this. No one in the organisation was allowed to issue an invitation to tender until they had attended the course and passed it. Even then, the first few tenders of his 50 graduates were subject to internal review before they were allowed out of the building.

➻ The author of the tender and the evaluator/marker of the submitted bids may well not be the same person. In big organisations people are routinely promoted, moved sideways or leave. If the evaluator is different from the author, he or she may well be faced with the same challenge that you have, of understanding and picking apart the component elements of a densely-constructed question. Playing back to them an equally opaque answer or set of answers compounds the problem. Remember also that the governance protocols of the client may require the reviewing panel to include a non-technical or lay person. If your submission is filled with industry jargon and unexplained acronyms, you're just raising barriers to their ability to grasp it.

5. Favouring style over substance and cheating the system

Formula 1 teams often push the boundaries to gain an advantage. Sometimes they overstep the mark of what is acceptable, with disastrous consequences ending in the loss of a Constructors' World Championship title. It's a very expensive error of judgement. By analogy, today's writers of bids are too often the unconscious victims of in-house publishing software that pushes the limits of what the marker believes is acceptable. This kind of software is meant to be a facilitator of productivity and efficiency, as well as ensuring the standardisation of written documents. Yet all too often, when it comes to bid writing, publishing programs adapted to incorporate the organisation's in-house style can impose an inflexible straitjacket on bid preparation and submission.

The problem can be made worse if the tender document has mandated strict page limits for uploading of bid submissions, and people within their organisation make the bid writer's job more difficult by insisting on inserting pointless, glitzy images which waste space. Rule this out. We also see another ruse employed in the submission of bids where the mandated space is restricted, or word limits are tight: bid writers or others attempt to beat the system by inserting into the document charts, tables and words in a smaller font size, usually in breach of the guidelines. If this is spotted by the assessor – and in many cases it is – non-compliant elements are excluded. In some cases the bid in its entirety may even be deemed to be non-compliant and excluded.

Even if bids of this type make it through initial assessment the assessor will be on the alert, and this may well impact on the way he or she approaches your submission. It will raise the question, if you cannot follow instructions, what will you be like as a contractor if you are awarded the project? Is this the norm for your organisation?

6. No added value included

Reliable statistics on bid submissions are hard to obtain and so from over a decade of experience, we estimate that the average number of responses to a business-to-business ITT is around 25, in some sectors lower, in some sectors higher. It's very rare to find that number drop to single figures. So you're in a competitive situation from the word go. Therefore, your bid needs to provide the evaluator with a reason to take your submission seriously. That means shortlisting **you**, which in turn means that your bid has to stand out from the crowd.

Thus, for example, if the client specifies urgent repairs within three hours, you may wish to offer two hours as an alternative, enhanced benefit. Propose the provision of a portal or app which can offer real-time tracking and monitoring of specific tasks. Bear in mind, however, that such offers may form part of the contract if awarded, and you will have to live up to your promises.

7. No evidence to support added value

A bid is basically a **sales document**. You are attempting to persuade the target customer to buy from you, and you need to provide reasons for them to buy. Imagine that you are on the other side of the table, being sold to. To commit to purchasing, especially if a large capital outlay is at stake, you would want to be convinced that you were making the right choice. This is not an impulse purchase, but a considered buying decision that follows a predetermined process. In making that decision you would wish to see compelling evidence to support the seller's claims and assertions and, even more to the point, if you work within a large organisation, it is more than likely that you would be expected to justify your decision to your colleagues or the people you report to.

It is not enough, then, to make assertions about the value that your bid would add to the project, if there is a lack of compelling evidence in support of this. Too often the bids that we review either make vague, unsupported claims that, frankly, any organisation bidding in the sector can make, or do not tailor the supporting evidence sufficiently to make their case. For example, simply copying and pasting unedited examples and case histories is rarely enough to do a convincing job. The materials you supply have to be matched to the specific requirements of the tender, just as the profiles of the delivery team you put forward have to fit with the client's needs.

Amateurs need not apply

"You cannot be serious!" Perhaps the best-known remark associated with tennis legend John McEnroe, in his long career of arguing with umpires over their decisions. It also aptly describes the attitude of a bidder displayed in an episode we witnessed first-hand.

Not long ago, those responsible for one of London's best-known public buildings embarked on an extensive programme of refurbishment. The project was valued at tens of millions of pounds and several major construction firms were invited to submit bids for the main contract. In view of the complexities involved, two pre-bid information evenings were scheduled, to which all potential bidders who expressed interest were invited. The sessions were complementary, jointly explaining the total picture: not just enlarging on the specifications of the project, but outlining the compliance required to respect the building's status as part of the UK's national heritage. Each session also offered opportunities for the audience to ask questions to clarify their understanding.

An organisation known to us was on the list of those invited. They failed to send a representative to the first session, but turned up for the second. At the end of the presentation, their [fairly junior] manager asked a question. "We can't answer that question," replied the presenter, adding somewhat acidly, "as you'd have known if you'd attended the presentation last week."

> The organisation concerned had not read and noted the briefing properly, and had failed to nominate a senior manager to be accountable and responsible for the bid. They submitted a bid anyway. Needless to say, they didn't make the shortlist.

Bear in mind also that the client may well check that your claims and assertions stand up to scrutiny. If they don't, it is possible that the contract, if awarded, could be terminated and you could be sued for breach of contract. Sounds unlikely? We are not just talking about statements relating to past projects. We know of a recent case where the delivery team specified in the successful bid did not match the team that actually managed the project. The contractor was sued and the tenderer was awarded damages. Read the small print carefully, especially if the project is to take place in a different jurisdiction from where you are based. An overseas court will typically find in favour of the home company. And an emerging trend is for some client organisations to require winning bidders to lodge tender bonds against future possible claims for breach of contract and consequential damages.

Forming the Bidding Team

I T IS BEST to look at the formation of the bidding team from two perspectives. First, there is the internal perspective. Who is required to fulfil the roles and responsibilities needed to put the bid together?

Second, there is the perspective of the target client. You need to present them with the most credible line-up that you can, bearing in mind that, should you make the shortlist, key members of the team will be representing you at any presentation you will be making. This is elaborated in Part III.

Here is our template for the formation of an effective bidding team:

- The *bid director* should have an ongoing overview of the bidding strategy of the organisation as a whole, and how each bid fits with this.

- The *bid manager* makes sure that the bid meets the specifications of the tender on time and in full.

- The *bid writer* originates, compiles and edits his or her own work and contributions from others.

- The *bid coordinator* acts as right-hand or wingman to the bid manager.

- The *operational person* is responsible for all internal administration and project delivery associated with the bid, from start to finish.

➟ The *critical friend/bid reviewer* sits outside the core team, and reviews the final draft before it leaves the building – the fresh pair of eyes.

➟ The roles of *estimator* and *planner* are self-explanatory.

➟ *Contractual* and *finance* expertise may be in-house in bigger organisations, or bought-in by small organisations: the important thing is to give the nominated individuals early sight of the tender, so they can help spot potential problems well in advance.

➟ *Specialist supply chain partners* may be required for a specific project.

➟ *Sales and/or Marketing manager* should be available to brief the team with up-to-the-minute market intelligence.

The strategy Kick-Start meeting

Observations on the bidding team

The bigger your organisation and the more important the bid, the more closely your bid team will resemble the ideal. But we live in the real world. Smaller organisations bidding for smaller projects often have to combine some of these roles in one person: that of the bid director and bid manager, for instance, or those of bid writer and bid coordinator, and estimator and planner. What matters is that by the end of the Kick-Start meeting each member of the team is clear about the role[s] they are going to play there and then, and thereafter as the process gets under way. A lack of clarity is a recipe for confusion further down the line and unnecessary errors will follow from this.

Let's return to our imaginary business. In Part I we showed the potential impact of a comprehensive, integrated bid writing strategy on the organisation's annual performance. Now let's review how changing the approach to the Kick-Start meeting can provide a smoother, more efficient process for creating and delivering a winning bid.

Picking the bidding team

Ideally, the composition of your team should include:

➤ Bid director.

➤ Bid manager.

➤ Bid writer/s.

➤ Bid coordinator/s.

➤ Operational person.

➤ Critical friend – bid reviewer.

➤ Estimator.

➤ Planner.

➤ Contractual expert.

➤ Finance expert.

➤ Specialist supply chain partners.

➤ Sales/Marketing manager – to supply relevant client intelligence in relation to the bid.

Key criteria

➤ Availability of the team who will deliver the project.

➤ *Relevant and similar* project experience.

➤ Individuals *who will be involved* in the project.

➤ People *who will give the client confidence.*

Case study exhibit B: How to manage the Kick-Start meeting - pre- and post-meeting

Before - Preparing for the Kick-Start: briefing materials for distribution

The more information that is circulated in advance, the better use you will make of the time available in the meeting. **The checklist below also serves as the agenda for the meeting**:

- Circulation list and meeting agenda.
- Raw tender documents from the client.
- Internal research summary.
- Information flowing from any mid-bid meetings.
- Tender clarifications, if appropriate.
- Information from similar past bids.
- Information from similar past bids *for the particular client.*
- List of core questions.
- Know and understand the scoring criteria.
- File naming protocol.
- Produce an agenda.

After - Actions flowing from the Kick-Start meeting

A thorough understanding of the project, to enable information to be disseminated as follows:

- Agreed bidding timetable.
- Agreed correct client name and any abbreviation to be used.
- Agreed who will raise and distribute any tender clarifications, if required.

➤ Agreed reference projects [e.g. case studies] and any previous bids that will be made use of.

➤ Agreed commitments to be made as part of the offer.

➤ Agree evidence for use.

➤ Allocate resources to individual tasks.

➤ Allocate lead author to individual question/s in the tender.

➤ Agree the meaning of individual questions.

➤ Agree the file name protocol – in compliance with client requirements.

➤ Check the page, word, or character allowance given against the questions – is this the same as that given in the scoring matrix? If there is a discrepancy, raise the issue with the client.

➤ Understand any appendices allowed: we find this is often unclear, so raise any grey areas early in the tender process, so you don't waste time working on how you *think* it might be, only to find that the client has a better, or at any rate different, idea!

➤ Allocate page allowances to match the scoring allocation.

➤ Create master answer template document.

➤ Provide an answer framework for each question, which is formatted to contain:

    ➤ The question

    ➤ The headings

    ➤ The scoring criteria

    ➤ Correct font type

    ➤ Correct font size

    ➤ Correct line spacing

    ➤ Correct margins

➼ Provide evidence.

➼ Agree the use of colour-coding.

➼ Key win themes: providing reasons to buy *from us*.

➼ Key messages: ditto.

➼ Agree the use of 'track & change'.

➼ Bid review process.

➼ Submission process.

Policy on version control

It's important to apply version control on all documents relating to a bid. We've found the best method is a fairly simple one:

➼ All active bid documents are allocated a version number [Vx] after the document title, together with the author's initials, e.g: **'Quality Processes Vɪ PBC'**.

➼ Each time the bid document changes a new version number is allocated.

➼ All previous version documents are archived for reference.

It is advisable to include this in the agenda of the Kick-Start meeting, as it is often the case that the tenderer mandates the file name protocol to be used in bid submissions. If so, everyone involved in contributing to the bid needs to follow the same naming conventions. Not only will this save time and avoid confusion, it also reduces the risk of non-compliance.

If this is not mandated in the tender document, then a protocol needs to be formally agreed and adopted at the meeting. Bear in mind the subfolder issue: if the file designation exceeds a certain character length, it may be rejected by a standard programming suite, such as Microsoft Word.

Writing Bids that Clients Want to Read

The golden rules

THERE ARE **THREE** golden rules that every winning bid adheres to. The bid has to be:

1. *Readable* by the client: easy to read by comparison with more turgid submissions.

2. *Scoreable* by the marker [assessor]: easy to assess in line with the client's specified metrics.

3. *Learnable* by the shortlister team: easy to memorise in terms of key points and features, for the interview.

1. Readable

We said above that in our experience the average number of bids submitted in response to an RFQ or ITT is about 25. A bid for a complex tender might well run to 40 pages or substantially more. That's an awful lot of documentation to get through. Your task, then, is twofold:

1. To avoid providing the assessor with reasons to eliminate your bid at first reading, by not making the basic errors we've already outlined [the Not-so Magnificent Seven].

2. To engage the assessor by making your bid simple and easy to read and digest.

We've already covered point one, so let's focus on what makes a bid simple and easy to read and digest.

First, you should strive as far as possible to write your submission in standard English, using short, direct sentences. Wherever you can, avoid technical jargon and anything that might be read as ambiguous or unclear. You cannot assume that the evaluator will always be an expert in the field, so take this into account.

Second, as we've already alluded to, the evaluator might not be a native English-speaker. If every third sentence makes them refer to a dictionary or consult a colleague, you're not winning any friends. That doesn't mean oversimplifying or talking down, but just keeping the language simple and direct.

Third, your bid needs to strike the right tone from the start, instilling confidence in the recipient that yours is the right organisation – indeed the obvious choice – for shortlisting. Words like "should" and "could" must be avoided in favour of "will" and "shall". In the office we refer to "should", "could", "maybe" and the like when we see them as *weasel words*. By that we mean they avoid commitment on the bidder's part. Evasive phrasing raises suspicions in the reader's mind. You should not be hesitant or evasive. You should be confident and committed. The more you present yourself as a serious contender, the more you will be regarded as a serious contender. Many clients, especially in the public sector, are very alert to this 'defraying' language.

2. Scoreable

Presented with many submissions, the evaluator will be seeking to score each bid that has made it through the first pass against the specified metrics. This is a relatively easy task when it comes to questions that demand a simple answer yes or no, or a factual statement such as the net worth of the bidder, that can be quickly verified. It's more onerous when it comes to unpacking the answers required by questions that are harder to answer. Here are two examples of how to address this in a bid submission.

Unpacking complex questions

Example 1 – A typical question

Question: Describe the processes, experience and resources you have available to ensure that projects are completed on time and to budget.

Your answer should specifically separate, address and evidence the points below:

Initial feasibility and validation of client requirements – Marks Allocation 10%

Site surveys and "abnormals" assessment – Marks Allocation 15%

Management of design – Marks Allocation 10%

Project planning and project management – Marks Allocation 20%

Cost management – Marks Allocation 20%

Site management – Marks Allocation 15%

Handover – Marks Allocation 10%

You have a Page Allowance of four A4 Pages

NB. A separate part of the scoring criteria in the tender stated that to achieve an "Excellent" score across all answers you must feature elements of added value.

This is the point at which to refer to the *Not-so Magnificent Seven Mistakes to Avoid*, as guidance on how to tackle the answer. To recap, these are:

1. **Not reading and adhering to the guidelines** – and so before you answer the question you need to have read the Tender Documents and formed your winning strategy

2. **Not answering the Question** – by including the headings as shown below you cannot miss answering the individual elements. The big issue is whether you have answered them correctly!

3. **Failing to allocate page, word or character allowance in proportion to the scoring criteria** – it is essential that you take the 4 x A4 pages allocation and relate this to the available marks, i.e. allocate the most time and space to the elements that have the greatest score. Just make sure that you still allow enough time to submit a compliant bid. You need to answer ALL questions.

4. **Unstructured Answers** – by following the same layout as the question you will make it easy for the marker to check you have answered every part and award you marks. Don't make the marker struggle!

5. **Favouring Style over substance and "cheating" the system** – your strategy meeting will have decided the use of Headers, Footers, Logos, Images, etc., in a controlled fashion. Always remember that the words are important and images are often used to make it look pretty! If you do use images, make sure that they are relevant.

6. **No Added Value included** – your strategy will have identified what added value you will deliver and at this point you make a commitment in writing. The heading should have been included from a thorough reading of the Tender Documents and included within your strategy for achieving the maximum marks.

7. **No evidence to support Added Value** – It is at this point you can propose how your added value will deliver client benefits. Don't forget that all clients want to know 'What's in it for me?' We have included a specific heading to bring this to the attention of the Marker and hopefully you are going one step further than your competitors!

And now on to the answer…

The headings should be structured as follows:

Answer

Ensuring projects are completed on time and to budget

This should be a short general introduction commentary and act as a lead-in to the main topics to be covered.

Headings feature each scoring element of the question posed, as follows:

1. Initial feasibility and validation of client requirements

Evidence:

2. Site surveys and "abnormals" assessment

Evidence:

3. Management of design

Evidence:

4. Project planning and project management

Evidence:

5. Cost management

Evidence:

6. Site management

Evidence:

7. Handover

Evidence:

Added Value:

Statement:

Client Benefits:

Statement:

Example 2: In this case, the tendering organisation has made clear what it considers to be an answer that scores the maximum ten points and is considered "Excellent".

Question: Please can you provide details of how your IT systems have supported the management/delivery of the services you have provided, or are currently providing, and how your clients are accessing this data.

10 – Excellent defined as: The response / evidence exceeds expectations and demonstrates clear and strong evidence of delivery as part of an integrated team and how this has become part of a continuous improvement process.

Again, we refer you to the *Not-so Magnificent Seven Mistakes to Avoid* as guidance on how to tackle the answer. These are:

1. **Not reading and adhering to the guidelines** – and so before you answer the question you need to have read the Tender Documents and formulated your winning strategy.

2. **Not answering the Question** – this time we have generated the headings [below] as part of our response, featuring the main issues to be covered, together with evidence.

3. **Failing to allocate page, word, character allowance in proportion to the scoring criteria** – this time there is no specified allowance and so part of your strategy is to properly cover the topics without writing too much or too little. We recommend that font size and style follow the client's Tender Docs.

4. **Unstructured Answers** – by following a logical sequence, you will make it easy for the Marker to award you marks.

5. **Favouring Style over substance and cheating the system** – your strategy meeting will have decided the use of Headers, Footers, Logos, images, etc., in a controlled fashion. Always remember that the words are important and images are generally used to make it look pretty!

6. **No Added Value included** – this question does not specifically ask for this. However, your strategy will have identified what added value you will deliver and at this point you make a commitment in writing.

7. **No evidence to support Added Value** – it is at this point you can propose how your added value will deliver client benefits…… don't forget that all clients want to know "What's in it for me?" We have included a specific heading to bring this to the attention of the marker and, we hope, you are going one step further than your competitors!

And now on to the answer…

The headings should be structured as follows:

Answer

Introduction to our IT Systems

This should be a piece about your systems and include:

➡ Investment

➡ Working in line with the Data Protection Act [soon to be GDPR: see Appendix 3]

➡ System security

➡ Business Continuity Planning

➡ How our IT systems have supported the management of our services

➡ How our IT systems have supported the delivery of our services

➡ How our clients have accessed this data

➡ Evidence of how we have exceeded expectations

➡ Evidence of delivery as part of an integrated team

➡ How this evolved to become part of a continuous improvement process

➡ Added value

Sample question 1 is typical of that which you will see in tenders. It's a single sentence of 20 words. Looked at like that, it's deceptively simple. When you put it under scrutiny, however, it's anything but. In reality it's a deep dive into how your business operates today and how it has operated in the past.

In response to this question, we've identified seven separate processes that need to be in play and explained, that will deliver a successful outcome to time, to budget and to specification. You might think these are obvious and don't need spelling out. You'd be wrong. The tender is asking you how serious and credible you are in relation to this project. If you can't satisfy the client, it's a fair bet that the competition will. Get it right and you've demonstrated your professionalism.

3. Learnable

We've observed that a bid is essentially a selling document. It can also be usefully seen as a **story**, or a vision of the future. From the earliest age we are enthralled by a compelling narrative; story-telling is one of the closest bonds that parents create with their children. As we grow older we graduate to books, films and TV as our sources of narrative to make sense of the world, and stories play a central role in our education and professional development. Law schools and business schools, to take two examples, make case histories and case studies a central part of many courses. It's not hard to see why. The particular illustrates the general. A good story remains in our minds long after the theory which it illustrates has been forgotten, but which recollection of the case brings vividly back to life: "So *that's* the point."

We are accustomed, then, since early childhood, to absorb and retain the lessons of life through the stories told to us. Often those stories have smaller stories, episodes, if you like, embedded within them. Thus, the most powerful bids are those which contain memorable case studies that both support the main storyline – why you should buy from *us* – and add life and colour to that narrative.

What makes a credible and compelling case study?

Case studies in your bid documents must be focused around reality; understand that the client may well check them out.

Dos

A *checklist of essential features* is listed below. The case study is usually best captured on one page. It must be relevant to the project you are bidding for and include important details such as:

→ Client name

→ Project name

→ Project description

→ Project value

→ Project duration

→ Added value provided

→ Benefits to client

→ Project narrative summary

→ Challenges overcome

Follow the client tender criteria specified, such as:

→ Project value

→ Project size

→ Must be a project completed within the last XX years

Don'ts

→ Don't use case studies that are dissimilar to those requested

→ Don't attach additional sales information

→ Don't refer to "additional information being available on request"!

→ Don't favour images at the expense of narrative

Every well-told and memorable written story has a beginning, a middle and an end. Along the way there will be signposts, cues and reminders to the reader, so that if he or she is interrupted, leaves the story and returns to it, they can pick up where they left off with the minimum of difficulty. It will also feature challenges that have been overcome. Part of the craft of every professional writer, be they journalist, advertising copywriter or bid writer, is to guide the reader seamlessly through the story, ideally without the reader consciously realising that their hand is being held. This is all the more important in bids that are longer and more complex. An important part of the designated bid reviewer's job is to put themselves in the shoes of a prospective reader and satisfy themselves that at no point would that person feel they have, quite literally, lost the plot.

Learnable by the shortlister team

We've examined learnability from the point of view of the reader, but the effective crafting of a good story will also help the team learn the bid and form the basis of the presentation. This is invaluable for shortlister meetings. What is the essence of the bid? What will this bid do for the client? How is it going to solve their problem? What makes **our** organisation the obvious choice of partner?

Let's also go back briefly to the Kick-Start meeting, and the preparation and process that we recommended. It might seem like a long to-do list, but you will see a massive pay-off when it comes to the team's ability to internalise the bid, and it will be particularly useful if team members are working simultaneously on other proposals. The initial documentation and any subsequent changes can be rapidly collated for ready reference, and any substitute team members can be handed the file to bring them quickly up to speed.

Gap analysis – undertaken by the designated bid reviewer

The **gap analysis** is our term for the roles and responsibilities of the internal bid reviewer designated in the Kick-Start meeting. The right person for the task is someone who really likes getting into detail and is happy to work through complex documentation. It's essentially an editorial function, and you're looking, therefore, for someone who is a) not a member of the team that put the bid together, and b) is meticulous and systematic in their approach.

➡ *Not a member of the bidding team*: if the bid reviewer is a part of the team that created the submission, you're effectively asking people to mark their own homework, which is never a good idea. You're also depriving yourself of the opportunity to have a fresh pair of eyes review the bid before it leaves the building.

➡ *Meticulous and systematic in their approach*: the bid reviewer is going to be comparing two documents: the original RFQ or ITT, and your organisation's response. He or she should be tasked with:

➡ Ensuring that the bid fully complies with all the tender requirements and guidelines, both in form and content.

➡ Cross-checking that all the questions raised are fully and appropriately answered.

➡ Confirming that all clarifications have been taken in to account in the answers.

➡ Confirming that the answer will achieve the highest-ranking score, i.e. excellent.

➡ Reading through supporting evidence to confirm that it is tailored to meet the particular circumstances of the tender, i.e. that it is timely and relevant.

The internal bid reviewer also needs the strength of character to stand their ground and argue their corner if the bid needs revision. If they meekly go along with whatever comes through the system, they're not adding the value that could make the difference between your organisation making the shortlist or being consigned to the also-ran pile.

Ideally the bid reviewer should recruit a second pair of eyes, just to check that they haven't been snow-blinded by the volume of documentation and missed something as a result. It can happen to even the most diligent reviewer. However, in smaller organisations, this is not always possible, which is yet another reason for starting with a targeted bidding strategy that doesn't create an overload.

Reviewing the Bid as it Evolves

NEITHER LARGE NOR small organisations benefit from cumbersome processes that absorb too much of everyone's time and are the source of resentment. To keep things tight while ensuring nothing falls between the cracks, we suggest you hold weekly bid review meetings.

Regular weekly bid review meetings

These meetings should be focused and short, and follow a standard agenda covering:

➤ Progress review

➤ Client changes to the submission date

➤ Tender clarifications

➤ Outstanding information

➤ Any issues arising that need resolving

➤ Date and time of next review meeting

Appoint someone as timekeeper and schedule two hours as an absolute maximum. If you finish early, to everyone's satisfaction, wind it up. Everyone will be grateful!

Review meeting attendees

The following key participants should be at the meetings:

- ➤ Bid director

- ➤ Bid manager

- ➤ Bid writer/s

- ➤ Bid coordinator/s

- ➤ Estimator

- ➤ Operative person

The process of reviewing what happens before your bid leaves the office is explained in the box opposite.

Bid reviewing process

The bid reviewing process needs to follow a simple yet effective quality review process and work at two levels:

Level 1: Critical friend/bid reviewer quality checks
This includes:

→ Does it answer the questions?

→ Have key themes been reflected?

→ Has the golden thread* been reflected throughout all answers?

→ Checking that the answers don't contradict each other.

→ Has the correct voice been used?

→ Remove any negative statements.

→ Remove any defraying language.

→ Check the evidence used is relevant to the answer.

Level 2: Standard bid document quality checklist
Please see Appendix 2.1.

* The golden thread consists of consistently mirroring throughout the bid the key concerns of the tenderer; thus if speed and consistency of delivery are critical, these should be picked up as a running theme in what we refer to as reinforcing statements.

How to Prepare for When You Make the Shortlist

CONGRATULATIONS! YOU'VE MADE the shortlist. As a result, along with all the other shortlisters, you will almost certainly be asked to make a presentation to the client organisation. An agenda will be circulated in advance, and your approach needs to reflect the client's requirements.

This is where the effort employed in making the bid *learnable* pays dividends. To have made the shortlist, it's almost certain that you've created a compelling story and a coherent narrative that make sense to the prospective client. In doing this you've fashioned a series of hooks on which your team can hang their pitch: a beginning, a middle and an end, and memorable supporting evidence which they can refer to if the opportunity arises during the interview. As there could be some lapse of time between the submission deadline and the shortlister interview, it's also easy for the bidding team to refresh their memories, especially if they're called in at short notice.

Perhaps even more importantly, you've automatically created a plan B. The unexpected happens. People quit, go sick, have holiday plans they're unable to change, or competing commitments. If events require you to make a substitution, a bid that's easy to learn means that anyone coming off the bench can master the brief that much more quickly. Your contingency is built in and will cause the minimum of disruption.

You can go into the meeting confident that a united team will sing from the same page, and that all members can respond to headline questions directed at them.

Classic mistakes to avoid at a shortlister interview

The interview
Failure to:

➻ Follow the client instructions.

➻ Attend the correct address for the interview, which then makes you late.

➻ Agree a dress code and turning up disheveled – meet up beforehand and check.

➻ Take the bid manager or operational person who will deliver the project.

➻ Read the bid submission in detail prior to the interview and insulting the client's intelligence when you try to hoof it.

Don't:

➻ Attend with people who are not mentioned in your bid.

➻ If you *have* to attend with new people, advise the client beforehand.

➻ Take a person from the sales department with you – it is often a requirement that you don't.

➻ Cut across people who are speaking.

➻ Neglect to create a Leave Behind document [Summary].

➻ Be unable/unprepared to answer panel questions.

Presentation

Make sure you:

➻ Allocate parts of the presentation to those best suited to deliver the topic.

➻ Rehearse the presentation.

➻ Orchestrate the presentation – identify who in the team will take charge of different parts of the presentation, reflecting their expertise and experience.

➻ Summarise your presentation.

➻ Arrive in time – you don't want to end up running and spending most of the interview wiping your brow and being stressed.

➻ Complete the presentation in the allocated time. Time yourselves when you practise. The client will often be counting you down out loud to make sure they stop you dead, so stop a few seconds ahead of time. Don't let them catch you out!

➻ Prepare the questions *you* want to ask.

Showing confidence

If you've made the shortlist, you should rightly have confidence in your abilities. Many people understandably feel nervous prior to attending a face-to-face meeting. It's perfectly natural, a combination of uncertainty about what might be thrown at you, and the adrenalin that's pumping through your system. The fact is that you're about to perform and, as many well-known actors have admitted, last-minute nerves come with the territory. A certain amount of nervousness is not such a bad thing. Your body is telling you that it is keyed up and ready to engage.

If you are fairly inexperienced in public speaking and making presentations, it may pay you to get some formal training. Warren Buffett, the world's most successful investor, and renowned businessman and philanthropist, is known for his abilities as a public speaker. The annual general meetings of the business he chairs, Berkshire Hathaway, last for days, and the star attraction is the address from the chairman. It takes hours and gets a standing ovation every time. Buffett is on record as saying that the best investment in his education he ever made was the money he spent on a Dale Carnegie Public Speaking course – and this from a man who attended Wharton and Columbia Business Schools. The Dale Carnegie certificate is the one that's displayed proudly on the walls of his office. And so if it's worked for Warren Buffett, perhaps investing in some training is worth consideration.

Before the interview

There are certain things you should bear in mind *before* the interview that will help you relax as the meeting progresses.

The panel will most probably have been assembled at short notice. This is particularly true of larger tenders, which are likely to impact across the client organisation. In these cases the panel will be composed of representatives from different business functions or divisions, plus external consultants. They will likely have disparate views, reflecting the business silos in which they operate. **They will not necessarily have the depth of knowledge of the tender documents which the bidding team possesses.** If you've done your homework and are properly prepared, you start with the advantage: you know more about the bid than the people on the other side of the table.

The client is likely to hand the presentation over to you. Your starting position of strength is enhanced if the client puts you in the driving seat by inviting you to present your case. From debriefing the bidders that we've worked with after their shortlister interviews, we know that this is what normally happens. Assuming it does, this presents you with a great opportunity to take control of the meeting, so seize it with both hands.

It won't help you, however, if you attempt to bore or bludgeon a client into appointing you, so your presentation needs to be concise and relevant. Thirty densely-worded PowerPoint slides that more or less repeat what is in your bid will not promote your case. Of course, your presentation does need to be *consistent* with your bid, but it should be the opening element in a dialogue, not a monologue where the audience struggle to get a word in edgeways while you commandeer all the time that's been set aside for the meeting. If you monopolise the conversation, you risk raising doubts in the client team's mind about whether you're able to answer more difficult or searching questions and have designed the presentation expressly to avoid this.

You can structure the presentation and the interview to your advantage by deciding in advance:

➻ The length and format of the presentation. In 15 to 20 minutes maximum you should be able to convey the essence of what is contained in your bid: your credentials to deliver the project, your approach, the management structure you will put in place, and the team that's been selected.

➻ The role of chairman, who leads the presenting team and controls the replies. It won't make a good impression if either everyone jumps in to answer a question or there's an embarrassed pause while members of the team look expectantly at each other.

➻ The key messages you wish to reinforce, already present in the bid. The stress here is on *key*: three or four points are more likely to resonate and remain with your audience than twice that number. Remember, the question and answer session that follows may well allow you the opportunity to build on these.

➻ Decide what you wish to leave behind: not a hard copy of the presentation, but one side of A4 paper, on which you stress a few memorable key messages you want to leave in the minds of the panel. Make sure they reiterate points made in your presentation. This is not the time to introduce something new and depart the room leaving behind the impression that this is a hastily-assembled, last-minute job.

- Who answers which questions. Anticipating the likely questions is a critical part of being properly prepared. It's part of the chairman's role to consult and identify in advance what these are likely to be and who in your team is best placed to answer.
- The questions that **you** may want to ask. Again, this falls to the chairman to prepare. If the chairman of the client team is doing their job properly, they'll ask whether you have any questions on your side. You should. Not only does asking questions demonstrate that you are fully on board with the project, it provides a means of engaging with the client team at a conversational level and forms the first block in building a relationship with them.
- The supporting evidence you will be using.

During the meeting

A major factor in inviting you to a shortlister meeting is so the client can meet and assess *the team that delivers the project*, not be faced with a persuasive marketing team they will never see again. We mentioned above that on occasions you may have to field substitutes, but it is vital that the majority of the team consists of the individuals nominated in your bid. Specifically the client team wants a good sense of:

- The key team members on your side they will be working with.
- The structure of your team and a sense of how well the members will work together.
- The logic of the responses from the team to questions asked in advance, and the quality of responses to quick-fire questions posed on the day.

You will also need to prepare for the difficult or not so immediately obvious questions that you may be asked, and have your answers ready.

What are the potential weaknesses in your organisation's profile or the submission which an astute client team could pick up on and challenge you with?

Interview questions

Questions that you might want to ask

Every bid is unique, but we've noted two generic questions you should ask that might assist you in your preparation:

→ Will the notified project start date be met?

→ Will the client brief remain substantially unchanged?

And toughies you should be prepared for!

Some curveballs or googlies that we've seen coming from the other side of the table over the years:

→ We have a comment from a third party that you are failing to deliver on your XX project.

→ We understand that your project manager is currently fully committed on your XX project and won't be available for the start of our project.

→ We have analysed your current workload and we believe you are overtrading.

→ We have received a comment from a third party saying that you have a number of payment disputes with your supply chain.

→ Will you hold your price for another year?

→ What discount would you offer if we increase the contract value?

Impact on scoring the bid

Many clients use the interview to moderate the overall score and thus the final decision on awarding the contract. If so, it's a requirement that they state this in the tender documents.

This moderation normally happens when the client finds a difference – positive or negative – between your written words and what they find from:

➤ The interview and presentation process.

➤ Visiting your offices.

➤ Visiting one or more of your projects.

➤ Taking additional case study references.

Since moderation can be both positive and negative, it is vital for you to reflect your practices accurately in what you say, without embellishment.

The Best and Final Offer

A FURTHER VARIATION ON the tender process is used increasingly for the award of major projects: the Best and Final Offer [BAFO]. The client issuing the tender receives bids in response to its invitation and creates a shortlist of contenders. In the normal scheme of things these organisations are asked for interview and, after reviewing both the submissions and the outcome of the interviews, the client decides to modify the tender requirements in line with BAFO rules.

The reasons for doing so are typically because the bids or the conversations have contained suggestions for improving the project: faster or cheaper delivery, for example, mitigating risks or producing more added value to the outcome. The client understandably seizes the opportunity to incorporate this into their thinking and the result is Best and Final Offers from shortlisted bidders.

To illustrate, let's look at a BAFO Case Study. In this case, the prize was a £200m Framework Contract, divided between two organisations and therefore worth £100m to each winner, paid as £20 million per annum over five years. The location of the work was Central London and the sector was Social Housing. Apart from the prestige of winning a flagship project, the project was weighted 60:40 in favour of Quality versus Price.

The bidding company in this case compiled a Bid/No Bid Form, which showed the project was an excellent fit with their history, reputation and strategy. If they won, they knew they could deliver the project.

The key strategic decisions then involved making an offer sufficiently competitive to make the shortlist, in the knowledge that the BAFO stage would require a redoubling of effort when everybody associated with the bid would be exhausted, plus a possible combination of additional benefits and reduced costs.

A decision was made to bid for the contract.

The BAFO stage documentation contained:

- A change in works order priority.

- A shortened programme period.

- Contractor use of the client's property for site accommodation.

- Linking together of other programmes of works.

- Shared resource between the two selected partner organisations.

- A change to the replacement windows specification.

BAFO bidders were asked to give specific attention to:

- Efficiencies.

- Value For Money.

- Innovation.

- Working in partnership.

The bidding organisation concerned was also asked to attend five separate meetings, one with all the project stakeholders, two with particular individuals and a further two with groups of managers from the client organisation. In their BAFO submission, the bidder identified a saving of 5% over the initial ITT and a potential 10% further saving over the five-year life of the project: they were confident of reducing the costs to the client of their share of the project by a minimum of £20m. Ten days after final bid submissions, they were notified that they had been successful.

When the costs were finally totalled, the bidding organisation had spent £85,000 on bidding for the project, of which £20,000 was spent on the BAFO submission, to secure £100 million of work. A full version of this case study appears as Appendix 2.2.

Site Visit[s]

A T ANY STAGE in the submission process, the client may well wish to organise a site visit to a project you are currently managing, or a visit to your offices. If this happens, take it seriously! You don't get a second chance to make a first impression. Visits are often scored and used as a critical part of any moderation of your bid.

We suggest the following:

→ If you think your offices are likely to be visited, stand outside the building well before any possible visit. How does it look from the point of view of a client arriving? Keep it tidy and ensure that all signage required by law is in place.

→ As soon as you know the date of the visit, circulate an invitation and get it into everyone's diary. Set it in stone!

→ If you know that key people will not be available at this time and date, advise the client as soon as possible. Make sure any replacements are properly briefed. They are not there to make up the numbers.

→ Send the client a map of how to find you or the site, with the full address and two contact numbers that they can use, in case one of you gets caught on the phone. This is in case they are running late and need to let you know, or they cannot find you. You need to have someone allocated to this who knows the local area and is able to provide clear instructions. Check any disabled access requirements or dietary preferences.

➼ Always have refreshments ready for people on arrival.

➼ Have people on hand ready to greet the client team. They may arrive in a staggered manner over ten minutes or so. Greet them and don't stand around in a *them and us* manner.

➼ At the start, appoint someone ready to pull everyone together, go through the housekeeping, showing them where the fire exits are and where the facilities are and take them around in a pre-planned route. Have this free of hazards as some of your visitors may need wheelchair access.

➼ Make sure any inappropriate images or confidential information on display are removed.

➼ If the target client wishes to visit a site of an existing client of yours, try to have a happy client on hand ready to say a few words.

This is the client's final opportunity to try before they buy, and your opportunity to impress with your planning and efficiency. Make the most of it!

Takeaways from Part II

➤ Note and avoid the common mistakes – the Not-so Magnificent Seven – that derail many bids at the outset.

➤ Invest in setting up your Kick-Start meeting the right way: it will pay off massively down the line, saving you time and duplicated effort.

➤ Have a robust, well-defined checking and review process in place from the start: make sure you're not marking your own homework!

➤ Always ensure your bid conforms to the three golden rules: *readable, scoreable, learnable.*

➤ Prepare thoroughly for the shortlister meeting: remember, you start from a position of strength and this is your opportunity to gain the edge over the competition.

➤ If you're invited to engage with a Best and Final Offer round, be clear from the start about the commitment, costs and benefits of participation.

➤ If the target client requests a visit to your offices or to the site of a current project, take this seriously: it's your final chance to make a lasting impression of why yours is the right organisation to deliver the contract.

PART III

REVIEW AND IMPROVE

Introduction

W̲ᴇ ꜱᴛᴀʀᴛ P̲ᴀʀᴛ III by summarising the key learning points from Parts I and II, which are the building blocks of better bid writing performance. Embed these seven essential elements in your organisation, and they will serve as a firm foundation on which to develop an enduring culture of continuous improvement, improving your win rates and creating that all-important sense of purpose and momentum.

Once these seven elements are a matter of routine, you can look to maintain your competitive edge by improvements at the margin. Observing how the best in class have done this provides valuable insights into what it takes to win, and win consistently. We link this to what we describe as *the view across the bridge*, that is to say the feedback we've collated from tendering organisations on what distinguishes a winning bid from an also-ran. To give you the most informed perspective of what tendering organisations are looking for, we've collated data from across the world over many years.

This sets the scene for the internal processes we recommend you implement to review your own bidding performance, both each bid individually and a collective review of your overall bidding process at regular intervals. These reviews feed into your bidding strategy, so you can modify this progressively if necessary. Many organisations confine their review process to bids they have failed to win. In our view this is a lost opportunity – we explain why you can often learn just as much by analysing the bids that you have won, and identifying the factors behind your success, so you can replicate these in future submissions.

A focused bidding strategy makes for a more efficient, less time-consuming reviewing process. It also creates time for some routine housekeeping tasks that are too often overlooked. Case studies and other supporting materials need to be regularly updated, archived and cross-referenced. Some material should, inevitably, be permanently consigned to the archives as no longer sufficiently relevant or recent. Emotional attachment can make this difficult to do, but regular spring-cleaning will put you in better shape to produce winning bids. Pay particular attention to identifying and recording examples of innovation in your past project delivery, especially where you can demonstrate tangible benefits to the client[s], such as a shortened cycle time, reduced cost or improved outcomes.

Key themes in Part III

➻ A culture of continuous improvement will contribute hugely to your long-term sustainability as a bid-winner. Even market leaders cannot rest on their laurels.

➻ Pay close attention to the seven building blocks of better bid writing. Implementing these and maintaining them in your organisation will make a major impact on your bidding performance.

➻ When you are satisfied that you have done the heavy lifting of basic improvements, then look for gains at the margins, to maintain your competitive edge.

➻ Make time and space available for review. A focused strategy, of bidding for fewer projects you are more likely to win, makes this possible.

➻ There are two review cycles: quarterly and for individual bids. Learn from your successes as well as your losses.

➻ Routine housekeeping, such as archiving and cross-referencing supporting evidence, may be unglamorous, but will make life easier for everyone involved in the bid writing process.

➻ Identify previous innovations resulting in tangible outcomes which the organisation has created, and record them. These could be the winning cards in your hand.

Recap: the Story so Far

BEFORE WE EMBARK on Part III, now is an excellent point to recap and summarise the key points of Parts I and II. These are the seven building blocks of better bid writing and, if you take nothing else from this book, we are confident that introducing these into your business will deliver financial benefits and continuous incremental improvements. These are summarised as follows, and presented in diagram form below.

1. Create a focused bid writing strategy, informed by market intelligence, which plays to your organisation's strengths and that fits with your overall business strategy.

2. Break down that strategy by three-month quarters, with clear targets for improving your bid writing performance.

3. Avoid the seven basic errors that derail so many bids at the outset, and screen each potential tender through a rigorous bid/no bid process.

4. Pick the team to match the requirements of each bid you decide to go for.

5. Set up a Kick-Start meeting to clarify roles, responsibilities and supporting processes.

6. At that meeting, define the bid review processes and ensure these are rigorously implemented.

7. Prepare thoroughly for the shortlister meeting and any associated site visits.

The building blocks of better bid writing

Aim for here
→

| Prepare for the Shortlister Meeting |
| Define Your Review Process |
| Kick-Start Meeting |
| Pick the Right Team |
| Avoid Basic Errors |
| Set Targets and Improvement Goals by Quarter |
| Develop a Clear Strategy |

Direction of travel ↑

→
Start here

Learning from the Best

I**F YOU'VE READ** this far, it's safe to assume two things:

1. You're committed to winning.

2. You subscribe to the view that there's always something new to learn.

Taking time to review and to learn from your experiences and those of others is of critical importance in developing any aspect of your business, including bid writing.

One book we've found highly influential in our thinking is *Performance at the Limit: Business Lessons from Formula One Motor Racing* [now in its third edition], by Professor Mark Jenkins, who blogs at www.f1professor. com/blog. Jenkins has followed top-level motorsport for many years, in parallel to his career as a strategy professor. *Performance at the Limit* is a portrait of an industry in which the stakes are huge and the competitive pressures correspondingly high. The book is full of insights, but the lesson which has struck us most forcefully is the relentless, compulsive obsession with detail in an environment where success or failure hinges on a split second. This obsession runs right through the industry's DNA, from initial design, through analysis of every component of a Formula One car, to improving wheel change times at pit-stops.

For instance, over the course of a typical Grand Prix weekend McLaren's racing team will capture more than a billion data points from the 200+ sensors located on each car for analysis in real-time and review back at McLaren HQ. As evidence of the transferability of know-how, in 2011

McLaren announced a five-year strategic partnership with pharmaceutical giant GlaxoSmithKline, to use that acquired expertise in big data management for drug research and development.

Performance at the limit translates into *improvement at the margins*. We think it's no accident that this philosophy has been adopted wholesale by other sports and embedded within them by top coaches such as Sir David Brailsford, Olympic cycling performance guru and manager of the most consistently successful cycle racing team of all time, Team Sky. Brailsford is reputed to have made over 1,000 changes to the machines, trackwear, training and dietary regimes of the athletes under his care in preparation for the London Olympics of 2012 and the Rio Olympics of 2016. A little tweak here, a minor adjustment there – but the cumulative effect was to create an outstanding medal-winning outcome in both sets of Games.

The evidence we've seen has led us to conclude that organisations which succeed *simply know more* than their competitors, and put what they know into practice. Our own approach to performance improvement is to focus first on getting the big things right, and *then* give our attention to getting better at the margins.

The *big things*, defined by the seven building blocks, are all key factors in enhancing your win rate and determining whether a tendering organisation will take your bid seriously. They are chiefly about defining and embedding a robust set of processes which preserve the organisation's knowledge, protect it against the vulnerability of staff departures and stop you from constantly reinventing the wheel. Attention to the *little things* will maintain your competitive edge and instill a culture of continuous improvement.

Much of the rest of this book is devoted to addressing those *little things* which, taken together, enhance your ability to create bids that win business.

The View Across the Bridge

W<small>E ARE GOING</small> to come shortly to what we've identified as best practice in reviewing your bidding performance, as the starting point for introducing improvements for the future.

Before we do so, it's worth spending a little time to reflect on the view from *across the bridge*, by which we mean the clients' view of bids they have received. We've collated the feedback that bidding organisations have encountered from their target clients over the years, and condensed it into Table 5. Ultimately it's the clients' opinions that matter, given that they're the paymasters.

Table 5: Good or best bidding practice as defined by client [tendering] organisations

Bid submission by section/ stage	Viewed positively [The Good]	Viewed negatively [The Bad and the Ugly]
General approach by bidder in their submission	Making commitments. Demonstrating early on an understanding of key issues and project outcomes. Presenting clearly strategies and solutions. Proving with evidence, not just making assertions.	Using weasel words and failing to make commitments. Playing back the brief and/or specification and showing no appreciation of key issues or outcomes. Asserting, but not providing evidence: "trust us" is not good enough!
Bidder experience and resources as outlined in the bid	Focusing on recent and relevant experience and capability. Being specific how these will contribute to the project they are bidding to win.	Listing past projects, without referencing details of management or structure. No links to the core team proposed for this project.
Project team expertise and proposed structure to manage the project	Team availability for this project. Fielding a suitably qualified team and having back-up in place. No single point of failure. Providing a structure that allocates roles, responsibilities and reporting processes.	No commitment to team availability. No rationale for team nominations. No provision if a team member is unavailable. Vagueness over roles and responsibilities.

Bid submission by section/ stage	Viewed positively [The Good]	Viewed negatively [The Bad and the Ugly]
Proposed methodology	Showing how this fits with the scope and scale of the project. Good match with team roles and responsibilities. Demonstrating compliance with all statutory and regulatory requirements. High levels of engagement and consultation planned. Providing added value and/or benefits.	No accountability for who in the team is responsible for specific aspects of delivery. Lots of generalities, few specifics. No clarity over reporting relationships. Non-compliant. Offering no obvious added value or other benefits.
Document presentation	Properly proof-read. No obvious signs of cut and paste. Clearly tabbed by section. Ensuring that all flow charts/Gantt charts/ process maps are easy to read and understand, and referenced.	Difficult to read and sloppily presented. Complex tables, hard to interpret. Too much verbiage when a chart or a short answer would do the job. Not referenced.
Shortlister or BAFO meetings	Bringing the core team to the meeting, headed up by a senior representative of the firm. All members of that team having a detailed knowledge of the brief and the bid. Project manager and the delivery team making the biggest contribution from the bid team side.	Not bringing the core delivery team. Having the senior manager dominate the conversation. Talking about the bidding company, not the project. Marketing team overpowering the meeting.

This list of client likes and dislikes is not an exhaustive one. There may be additional things to consider that are specific to your market sector, but as a general overview it should serve as a handy reference guide when you try to see your bid from their point of view. It reiterates much of what we've already put forward in Parts I and II, for which we make no apology. As you begin your review process, ask yourself: "How much of what we did conforms to column 2 as opposed to column 3"?

An alternative way of thinking about the views expressed and collated in Table 5 is to group these under the headings of *Risk* and *Credibility*.

Risk

The perfect project can be characterised as *no unplanned events*. Where there are no unplanned events, the risks associated with delivery are either eliminated or minimised through contingency planning. If we walk through the bid cycle by the stages or sections shown in Table 5, we can see that a large part of the concerns expressed relate to the elimination or mitigation of risk.

At the start, the client wants to be assured that the bidder understands what this project is all about, and that this understanding is conveyed through the strategies and solutions proposed. If this reassurance is clear, any anxiety levels will start to fall. They'll drop further if the core team proposed look like the right people for the job, they're committed to the project and they're fitted into an organisational structure that makes sense. Concerns about risk are further mitigated if there's a squad of subs on the bench ready to take to the field if one of the players has to leave it. There's additional comfort for the client if the team knows the rules of the game and is committed to playing by them: the statutory and regulatory requirements.

These are all, so to speak, issues of substance, but they can be undermined by poor quality presentation. We've seen too many promising bids let down by slapdash documentation which is at odds with the image of professionalism others have worked hard to achieve. In a competitive market, there are no shortcuts. Everything has to hang together.

Credibility

Risk is what the client perceives from their side of the bridge. Things very rarely go exactly according to plan, so some residual concerns over risk are likely to remain in the client's mind. Credibility is what you, the bidder, are seeking to build as a means of countering that perception.

Look at the Bad and Ugly items listed in column three. If these sins of omission or commission don't actually destroy the bidder's credibility, they certainly don't enhance it. How can this bidder be serious if they simply rehash the brief and their basic pitch is "trust us"? There's either no specific supporting evidence, or materials that are outdated and irrelevant, a team that seems to have been chosen around who happened to be in the office at the time, indecipherable charts and, in the unlikely event they get to interview, a company director who knows nothing about the bid and does all the talking.

Would you want to buy from a business like this? Would you have confidence that they could make good their promises and deliver in full, on time and on budget? We certainly wouldn't!

It might be countered that these observations are concerned with perception, not underlying reality. Perception isn't necessarily everything but it counts for a huge amount.

Reviewing Your Wins and Losses

IMPROVING YOUR PERFORMANCE is dependent on taking time out to create an effective review process. The cycle of strategy formulation and performance review is shown below, broken down into four interlocking stages. Stages one and two were set out in Part I. Stages three and four are described in this section, Part III.

The quarterly process of review consists of grouping and listing your bid wins and losses at the end of each quarter. Reviewing your losses is standard practice for many businesses. But we rarely see businesses that systematically weigh up the costs of their losses against the value of their wins. This is confronting the reality of how well you're doing and provides, if you like, a balance sheet of your performance at any one moment in a time.

In fact, reviewing your wins is in general less common: most businesses seem to take the view that, after all, they were successful: why not just celebrate the fact and crack on with delivering the project? We suggest that **not** reviewing why you won is to miss a golden opportunity. Did you just get lucky? Was the field of competitors particularly weak? Or was it something specific about your business, your bid submission, or your shortlister interview that the reviewer[s] liked? Did a site visit to your premises or a current project you are working on tip the balance in your favour? The truth, of course, is that you may never know the answer for certain, but if you don't even ask the questions you're guaranteed to remain permanently in the zone of speculation. If you know **why** you succeeded, particularly because of something that you did, that success can be reinforced and repeated in future bids.

From a commercial point of view, simply creating a scorecard of wins and losses makes sense. Wins deliver revenue, losses don't. But it's important also to capture your successes [or failures] in making the shortlist. If we think of improvement as a journey, for many organisations making the shortlist more frequently is an important staging-post along the road and could be the first sign that their bidding performance is getting better. Improving shortlister success rates could even be a quarterly target that is set and measured.

Bid writing Quarterly Review Process

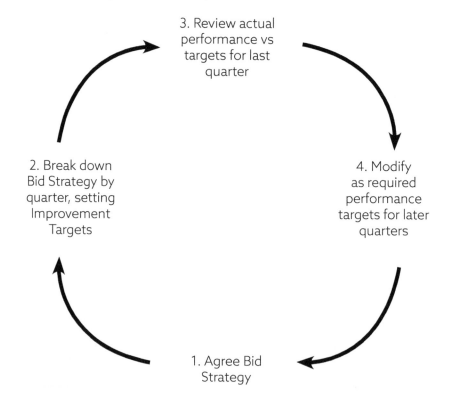

3. Review actual performance vs targets for last quarter

2. Break down Bid Strategy by quarter, setting Improvement Targets

4. Modify as required performance targets for later quarters

1. Agree Bid Strategy

Quarterly improvement

Allowing for delayed bid awards, you will know soon enough whether or not you have met your quarterly improvement targets. The next stage, then, is to find out why. When the data are gathered, start to look for external patterns. We have found the most influential patterns affecting bidding performance over an extended period to be:

➻ **Biases and trends:** Is there any bias or trend you can spot in terms of market sector or client type, that seems to correlate with your shortlister success or win rates? Market sector could be defined by geography – some clients just prefer to contract with a bidder that is local. Alternatively, sometimes distance makes no difference: what clients are looking for seems to be demonstrable expertise and track record in their sector, regardless of where the bidder is located.

➻ **Client size:** Does the size of the client play a part? Big organisations often feel more inclined to deal with other big organisations, and smaller organisations with contractors of a similar size. The commercial considerations of not having all your eggs in one basket come into play, but there is also the comfort factor of dealing with an organisation that is like your own.

➻ **Importance of project success:** The higher the profile of the project, the more people's reputations [and probable career prospects] are on the line – and the more risk-averse they are likely to be. In these cases, tendering organisations will be inclined towards a safe bet, and if you can't make a convincing case that this is what you are, you're unlikely to be in contention.

One issue to think carefully about is how frequently you should modify your targets. This needs to be approached with caution, especially if your industry sector is one where contract awards are often subject to delay. Don't be too quick to change when the picture of how you performed is still unclear. Sometimes it makes better sense to hold on and plan to make changes on a six-monthly basis, rather than jump to premature conclusions before you know the full results.

Review process for individual bids

The ideal review process for individual bids mirrors the bidding process. That is to say, you walk through the stages of creating and submitting each bid, as well as the outcomes once it leaves the building. As a process, we can represent this in simple form as follows:

➻ A: Create the bid > Review the bid > Submit the bid > Prepare for shortlist > Shortlist interview > [Site visit] > Win the tender*

➻ B: Create the bid > Review the bid > Submit the bid > Prepare for shortlist > Shortlist interview > [Site visit] > Lose the tender*[5]

➻ C: Create the bid > Review the bid > Submit the bid > Not shortlisted > Fail to win

As we mentioned in Part II, the site visit may take place at any stage of the process.

*May be extended, if subject to BAFO as described in Part II.

Essentially there are three outcomes we are interested in:

➻ Outcome A is the full success of winning the tender.

➻ Outcome B is when you make the shortlist but don't win the bid. However, there is useful learning for next time!

➻ Outcome C is when your bid fails to make the shortlist.

For each bid, we can expand this as shown in Table 6.

---

5   It is possible on occasions to challenge the award of a tender to a rival bid under the "Alcatel period" rules, explained in Appendix 2.2. Initiating this does, however, need careful thought and almost certainly legal advice from a specialist.

Bid review process – first stage

Table 6: Mapping the review process

	Internal		External				
Stage	Create the bid	Review & finalise the bid	Submit the bid	Prepare for Shortlist & possibly BAFO	Interview	[Site visit]	Win
Outcome							
A	✓	✓	✓	✓	✓	[✓]	✓
B	✓	✓	✓	✓	✓	[✓]	✗
C	✓	✓	✓	✗	✗	✗	✗

You start by looking at the internal stages. What did you do right or wrong that boosted or decreased your chances of success? Was it an appropriate tender to bid for, or was this, with the benefit of hindsight, always going to be a long shot? Looked at dispassionately, was yours a credible bid in view of the likely competition? Were the processes of creation, review and submission robust and, more importantly, were they followed? Did internal communications flow smoothly? These are the dice-loading factors that are under your control as an organisation.

Subject to the size of your organisation, this process should be headed up by either the bid director or the organisation's commercial director. The more bids you have to review, the bigger the scale of the task. The strategy of focusing on fewer bids that you stand a better chance of winning, which we outlined in Part I, will help you by making this process easier to manage.

Many people find it easiest to visualise this as a process map and sketch it as in Table 6, then comment on what you conclude about each stage of the process.

Bid review process – second stage

Once you have made your submission the bid has left your direct control, although there are still opportunities to influence the outcome if you've made the shortlist and/or the client has requested a site visit. The conclusions you've reached about how and why you performed as you did should be considered as tentative until you've requested and received feedback from the target client.

It's not always easy to get useful feedback on tenders you have bid for. The box below provides some guidelines on how to maximise your chances of getting a positive and helpful response to such requests.

The feedback you ask for and receive may not coincide with your own perceptions of how you did. It is not unusual, for example, for a bidder to find that a client says their bid failed to include something which you [the bidder] did. There is then a danger that the bidder's automatic conclusion is that it is the client's fault: the reader was lazy or incompetent.

In reality it may be symptomatic of a failure in the submission to give sufficient emphasis to one aspect of the tender, which can be addressed in future bids. If the recipient has not picked up a specific point made within the bid, the lesson to be learnt could be the value of using headings that signal the information clearly to the reader.

How to improve your chances of obtaining useful feedback on projects you've bid for

Ask for a face-to-face meeting: This may not always be possible, but this is often more use than just settling for a written response. You are able to ask questions that generate a dialogue. The answers can only be as good as the questions posed, so prepare thoroughly. If granted a meeting, go in the spirit of improvement, not recrimination. You are looking for clues that will help you write a better bid next time.

If you're not granted a face-to-face meeting:

➼ Make it easy for the other person to reply to a request. Ask short, specific questions that are simple to understand and answer. Remember that few people enjoy giving bad news. You're better off asking "How could we do better next time?" than "What did we do wrong?". In all likelihood you'll be told the same information, but your chances of getting a useful response are better.

➼ Also ask for feedback on what you did well.

➼ Be respectful in your tone, not accusatory. You are asking someone to take time out to do you a favour. You're more likely to get a result by asking nicely.

➼ Don't let your request look like a standard form your organisation routinely sends out. Make it personal and professional. Proof-read it before sending.

➼ If you can possibly offer the recipient something in return – **not** cash! – but which is relevant and useful, do so. A link to an authoritative commentary on their market that you have spotted on the web would be a good example.

➼ Follow up in person if you need to. Don't delegate this to a member of the support staff.

➼ Remember that you have the chance to impress the client and you may pick up work if the chosen contractor fails.

How to Capture What You've Learned

A FTER YOU'VE GLEANED whatever useful feedback you can obtain from the target client, next on the list is sharing this with the bidding team as soon as you can, while it is fresh in people's minds, so that everyone is in the picture.

The best way to do this is in a short, face-to-face meeting, with as many members of the team present as possible. If you have won the bid, it's a great opportunity to celebrate success and to thank everyone who contributed to that success.

Wherever you can, avoid sharing feedback by email or internal memo, certainly in those cases where you have failed to win. Emails too often provide a perfect breeding-ground for internal politicking, finger-pointing and point-scoring, when the whole point of the exercise is to learn and build upon your strengths whilst addressing your weaknesses. If some people cannot attend, you can always circulate the key outcomes of the meeting to them afterwards.

Structure of the meeting

No one likes to spend their time in unnecessary meetings, so keep these short and to the point. Your aim is threefold:

1. To share your internal analysis.

2. To present feedback from the target client, and comment on how and where that agrees or conflicts with your own analysis.

3. To discuss and reach conclusions about how you can improve your performance next time round, by building on your strengths and addressing your weaknesses: how can we do [even] better?

Engage the Sales and Marketing team[s]

Representatives from these functions should be present at the meeting. As a result of what you have learned, discuss key commercial targets and whether these can still be achieved. If necessary, reorganise your bidding priorities and update your forward planning accordingly.

The Review Presentation template below provides a concise way of presenting your conclusions regarding separate internal analysis and external feedback. In your text, use colour-coding to differentiate clearly between internal analysis and client feedback.

Review presentation template: How did we do?

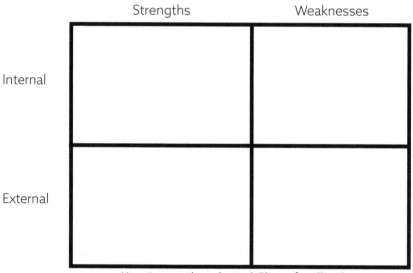

Key: Internal analysis / Client feedback

Housekeeping

Purposely limiting the number of bids you go for allows the organisation time for some routine, but very useful, housekeeping, as part of continuous improvement. We refer to this as *improvement at the margins*. Here are some key tasks that will deliver significant returns on your investment in time and effort.

Maintaining a library of information using version control and keeping it up to date

There's nothing more frustrating than knowing there's something your organisation did in the past that perfectly demonstrates your credentials for the project you're bidding to win – and then being unable to lay your hands on it. We've seen it too many times. Eventually someone in the office says "Fred – or Bill or Surinder or whoever – will know." Sure they do. Unfortunately they left the business last year/emigrated/retired and no one thought to document that knowledge for posterity. Perhaps there's something in the files, if you have half a day to rummage around looking for it. Organisational memory fades fast.

But let's suppose you are fortunate and the information you're seeking comes to light. More often than not there are multiple versions of the bid as work in progress, and no formal review of the project once it was completed. If you work through the files you can probably reconstruct what happened and the outcomes, but you're not a historian or a qualified archivist [actually, for firms that reach a certain size, there's a strong case for hiring a professional archivist to organise and structure the organisational memory]. That's why we suggested in Part II that you agree at the Kick-Start meeting a standard form of version control, not just for the bid you are working on, but for future reference. If you don't already do this, start now!

File under headings

This is so that vital information, such as case studies, can be easily retrieved. Depending on the resources available to you, you might want to create a proper relational database and the software you already use may allow you to do that quickly and inexpensively. But ambitious IT projects have a habit of taking twice as long and costing twice as much as planned, and ultimately failing to deliver their objectives. You may be better off with a quick and dirty approach – for instance a simple two-dimensional matrix which files all vital information under location [regional, national or international, subject to the scale of your business activities] and industry sector [e.g. healthcare, education, infrastructure, and so on]. If this creates a certain amount of duplication, so be it: you want to retrieve the appropriate material as fast as possible. It is more important to prioritise effectiveness over efficiency.

The most widely used materials in support of bids are case studies or histories. In Part II we advised against just copying and pasting unmodified versions of existing documentation. The old days of creating a standard case study and reusing it unaltered multiple times are long since gone. You have to assume that today's tendering organisations, both public and private, are sophisticated buyers, and respond accordingly. If you don't, your competitors will. The materials you supply need to be relevant and customised to the particular tender in question. Which brings us on to…

Retiring out-of-date documents

This is often quite hard to do. People in the organisation are understandably proud of great work that the business has done in the past. It may well have built its reputation on this, to which some senior managers owe their career success. Those who have been in the business a long time are likely to treasure fond memories of such projects. There is rightly a lot of emotional attachment involved, and the temptation of dusting down old favourites and recycling them is hard to resist. But as the years slip past a new generation takes up the reins. A target client is not just buying your organisation's past; it's buying its future. What your firm did 20 years ago might be very impressive, but what matters to *me* is what can you do for me *today*?

By all means make reference to iconic projects of yesteryear, but centre stage should be reserved for supporting evidence that is recent and relevant. Unless a specific timeframe is provided by the target client, we normally recommend using projects and other supporting evidence no more than three years old, or at a maximum of five years for an iconic project.

Retiring out-of-date documentation also applies to internal systems or processes which have failed to keep pace with the growth of the organisation. Sometimes the bid submission process brings this to a head, as the team finds it has to work *around* internal procedures rather than with them. What works for a £500k business is unlikely to suit a £5m business, and certainly not a £50m or £500m business. If the procedures are obsolete, they're an impediment to operating efficiently or effectively. Bring this to the attention of senior management and push for change!

Capture and record innovation

Experience tells us that evidence of the organisation's ability to innovate and bring fresh thinking to market can be a decisive factor in winning certain bids. Fresh thinking can take many forms: saving costs by doing things differently while achieving the specified outcome, for example;

deploying a new technology developed in-house; taking a technology developed in or for another market, adapting it and redeploying it; compressing a timescale through eliminating redundant processes. It often takes an outsider, however, to appreciate the added value that the ability to innovate creates and its wider application. It's even more valuable if past innovations come with IP rights or specialist know-how. In too many cases over time, the organisation just takes this for granted, rather than seeing it as a unique advantage in the sales armoury.

Trawl your organisation, then, for innovations that the business has brought to market, and record these. There is frequently an opening to integrate this aspect of your organisation into updated case histories and studies. Make sure you don't miss the opportunity.

Takeaways from Part III

- ➤ A culture of continuous improvement will contribute hugely to your long-term sustainability. Even market leaders cannot rest on their laurels.

- ➤ Pay close attention to the seven building blocks. Implementing these in your organisation will make a major impact on your bidding performance.

- ➤ When you are satisfied that you have done the heavy lifting of basic improvements, then look for gains at the margins, to maintain your competitive edge.

- ➤ Make time and space available for review. A focused strategy, of bidding for fewer projects you are more likely to win, makes this possible.

- ➤ There are two review cycles: quarterly and for individual bids. Learn from your successes as well as your losses.

- ➤ Routine housekeeping, such as archiving and cross-referencing supporting evidence, may be unglamorous, but will make life easier for everyone involved in the bid writing process.

- ➤ Identify innovations the organisation has created and record them. These could be the winning cards in your hand.

Parts I to III have concentrated on the state of competitive tendering as it currently stands. In Part IV, we share with you our insights into the world of tomorrow. Fasten your seatbelts!

PART IV

A GLIMPSE OF THE FUTURE

Introduction

"Prediction is very difficult, especially about the future."

— attributed to Danish physicist Niels Bohr

So far in this book we have concentrated on how you can improve your bidding performance in public and private procurement as the sectors currently stand. However, markets do not remain static. The pace of change is constantly accelerating, driven by technology, the economic cycle and the agenda of governments responding to shifting demographics and the needs of their citizens. These factors fundamentally shape the way business is transacted, and tendering for projects is no more insulated from change than any other commercial activity.

In this final section we share our thoughts on what the future will look like from the perspective of businesses that earn their bread and butter from winning contracts. We foresee three big drivers of change:

1. The diffusion of the internet of things from the domestic sphere into the built infrastructure and more widely across all commercial sectors of the economy.

2. Accompanying this, the interconnectedness of every aspect of business activity through multiple web-enabled platforms.

3. The need to maintain the integrity of this increasingly integrated network of communication, in which everything talks to everything else.

The challenges this new world poses for bidders are huge, but not insurmountable. Those businesses that emerge in the winners' camp will be those that can innovate to the benefit of their customers, nurturing a culture of continuous improvement, and those who are able to define and demonstrate clarity of business purpose.

The Lessons of History

HISTORY TELL US that some changes are incremental – they creep up on us little by little until one day what was once a radical innovation, like the smartphone, has become the norm. We only recognise the full extent of the change when we reflect on it over a long period of time. In the mid-1980s, for example, if you had predicted that within a quarter century IBM would be out of the hardware business and a virtually unknown software firm would be the world's most valuable company, you'd have been advised to lie down in a dark room until this aberration passed. However, the PC revolution swept across the world and none of IBM's increasingly desperate attempts to reinvent itself proved successful. Today it's essentially a consulting firm. Microsoft and Apple bet on a new and very different future, and they were right.

Other change is more abrupt and disruptive: Uber and Airbnb have transformed the taxi and tourism sectors almost overnight, creating enormous challenges for existing players. As for the threat posed to the traditional automotive industry by electric car innovators like Elon Musk [founder of Tesla]…we'll come back to that later.

In Part IV we share with you our own thinking about the future of bid writing, informed by the changes we see in the marketplace, by keeping our ear to the ground and by continuous conversations we have with people who are actively shaping the future.

When you get into the business of prediction you face two big challenges: picking out from the noise the forces that are really going to have an impact, and the timescale in which they take effect. If a Nobel prize-winner flags up just how hard this can be, it's wise to approach this ambition with a certain degree of humility. After all, the professional pundits were almost universally wrong about the outcome of the 2016 US Presidential election and the British electorate voting by a majority to leave the European Union!

Three Big Things to Think About and Plan For

Tʜᴀᴛ ꜱᴀɪᴅ, ᴡᴇ'ʀᴇ prepared to put down a marker that three big things are coming down the line and will have a radical impact on bidding for tenders.

1. The internet of things

The internet of things is much-heralded but until recently most of the focus has been on the effect this will have on the home: intelligent fridges that automatically reorder household staples when they're running low, temperature-control systems that can be remotely enabled and controlled through smartphones, sensors and meters that monitor and regulate energy consumption, and so on. Much of this innovation has been available for some time, and you are probably using aspects of it already in your own home. It's a fair bet that as costs go down and more players enter the market, the rate of adoption will increase and that within a few years most new homes will incorporate such technologies as standard.

But far less attention has been paid to the internet of things *outside* the home. Yes, we have seen the emergence of intelligent buildings that incorporate new technologies, but imagine an entire infrastructure comprised of components that are chipped and uniquely tagged: bridges, roads, urban transportation networks, schools, hospitals – a built environment that is intelligent from end to end, and in which every element can alert those who need to know when servicing, maintenance or replacement are required. Forget reliance on-site inspections or remote monitoring via CCTV cameras. The bridge will tell you when it needs some tender loving care. Each part will no longer be a *dumb* object, but classed and inventoried as an asset. Thick as a brick? Not in the future.

This might sound fanciful, but it's already on its way. In the UK, two major initiatives are underpinning this new world: *Building Information Modelling* [BIM] and *Digital Built Britain* [DBB]. BIM determines how the built environment is designed at the outset of a project, to incorporate new technologies, not bolt them on as an afterthought. DBB defines the end goal. At a recent conference hosted by the Royal Institution of Chartered Surveyors, the speaker in the closing address linked them together as follows:

> Over the next decade this technology [Building Information Modelling] will combine with the internet of things (providing sensors and other information), advanced data analytics and the digital economy to enable us to plan new infrastructure more effectively, build it at lower cost and operate and maintain it more efficiently. Above all, it will enable citizens to make better use of the infrastructure we already have.

Much of this thinking already underpins massive infrastructure renewal projects such as Crossrail in London and new urban transportation systems in New York City. The same philosophy is a major consideration for planners all around the world, particularly in the Far and Middle East, where more opportunity exists to leapfrog the legacies of 19th and 20th century design and employ the techniques of the 21st. But there is a particular urgency to drive this agenda forward in Britain, a crowded island with an ageing infrastructure and an expanding population.

2. The drive to raise productivity

In simple terms, this translates into getting more out of what you have or, even more desirable, getting more out of even less: more, longer trains on the existing rail network, fewer delays on current motorways, better utilisation of the health service, and so forth. Again, much of the attention has been devoted to the built infrastructure, mainly because of its enormous significance in the world economy. It is estimated that 13% of global GDP is spent annually on construction projects, while productivity in the sector has increased by only 1% per annum.

To quote Andrew Sentance, Senior Economic Adviser at PwC:

> All the G7 countries have experienced a sharp productivity slowdown since the financial crisis. Germany has seen no increase in productivity over the last 10 years and, in Italy, output per worker has been falling on average by -0.2 pc a year. Even the US… has seen less than 1 pc annual productivity growth since 2006.

At the same conference we referred to above, it was estimated that the UK construction industry could raise its productivity game *by between 50% and 60%* through changing its practices and by widespread adoption of the digital technologies embodied in the BIM and DBB initiatives.

Productivity in the UK, however you measure it, is a puzzle that has challenged economists and policy-makers for a long time. Viewed as a nation, the UK doesn't produce enough and it doesn't do so efficiently enough. It lags well behind other major economies such as the US, Germany and France. Various factors have been cited to explain this: a lack of investment, poor management practices, a workforce that lacks adequate skills, and the dominance of the services sector. None has so far proved to be the clinching argument and in a way a search for *the* reason matters less than the emerging consensus that action needs to be taken across the piece. The dawn of the digital economy provides arguably the best opportunity so far for transforming the situation. This isn't a partisan issue, either. All shades of government, trade bodies and professional associations are [rarely] in agreement: action needs to be taken, and it needs to happen now. It matters because without increases in productivity, real wages remain static or even go backwards, and so do living standards.

In the past, the instinctive tendency of governments was to spend their way out of the problem, either through increased borrowing or raising taxes. That's no longer the easy solution. In many economies structural deficits are already terrifyingly large – the total debt of the UK alone in mid-2017 was over 80% of GDP [gross domestic product]. The more you borrow, the higher the interest bill, to a point where you need to raise taxes just to service the interest payments. The fact is that very few of us actively want to pay more tax, and we're not inclined to vote for a political party that promises to increase the taxes we pay. Government is in a fix unless it can make every taxpayer's pound, dollar and euro work harder.

3. Security of data

Underlying points one and two is interconnectedness. You can't have an internet of things and a digital economy that raises productivity unless everything talks to everything else, across multiple platforms. We're already mostly there, and with depressing regularity we have witnessed the adverse consequences of the free mobility of information, from the rash tweet to the concerted attack on public and corporate IT systems by organised crime and even the teenage hacker in his bedroom. Once the genie is out of the bottle it's impossible to put it back. Information technology may be the great enabler, but it's also our greatest point of vulnerability. Informed sources warn that those intelligent devices in the home we mentioned earlier could be used as access points to infiltrate and infect your IT with malware. Even the security services are, so to speak, constantly playing catch-up to stay one step ahead.

The weakest link in the chain is where attackers will strike. The only long-term solution is to have no weak links in the chain.

Implications for Bid Writing

WHAT ARE THE implications of this vision of the future for bid writing?

The first is that *nice to have* will progressively turn into *must have*. We'd be foolish to state a precise date and, in any case, change of this kind is a process, not an event. Even hazarding a timescale is a challenge. Bill Gates observed that people tend to *overestimate* the impact of change within three years, and *underestimate* its impact over ten years.

Reverting to the case of electric cars illustrates this perfectly. They've been around for well over a decade, first as hybrids, then as all-electric vehicles. Only recently have the enabling technologies progressed to a point where these vehicles are now a mainstream proposition. At the time of writing, the maverick that was Tesla is more highly valued by the stock market than Ford. When Volvo announced in July 2017 that their entire automotive range would feature all-electric models within two years, the world woke up. Others have followed. The UK and French governments have announced plans to phase out internal combustion vehicles by 2040, and Norway has pledged to do so in less than a decade. Many commentators predict that once electric vehicles achieve price parity, which is almost upon us, consumer take-up will rise drastically and the transition from fossil fuels will happen even faster than governments plan for. The teenagers of today will be the users of battery-powered driverless cars tomorrow.

After all the hype and scepticism, the future has finally arrived: nice to have has indeed become must have and ten years from now, obeying Bill Gates' dictum, the automotive landscape will look dramatically different.

In terms of bid writing, the imminent arrival of the future means that all those in the food chain will have to be able to demonstrate that they can meet the requirements of interconnectedness, productivity gains and IT security. Those criteria will be passed down from main contractors to their subcontractors. This new world is coming down the line faster than many realise. For example, all bidders, both UK and overseas, will be required to show that they comply where necessary with the provisions of the General Data Protection Regulation, in force from May 2018 [see Appendix 3]. The bar is going to be raised and if you can't meet it, bad luck.

And for many contractors the mix of skills and competences required to win bids will alter dramatically. In certain sectors, notably social housing, the capabilities offered by new software packages have increased the feasibility for many providers of doing in-house what they used to put out to tender. To convince such organisations that they still need to issue tenders for the services concerned, bidders will have to demonstrate that they can bring something to the party, such as research-based innovation, which adds value. The rules of Darwinian selection will apply and if you want to survive, you need to evolve. Muddling through is not an option. Start planning now.

Second, though we have used as our example the construction sector because of its sheer size and economic importance, the impact of these new imperatives will be felt across the board. *Good practice* and *best practice* rapidly diffuse themselves across different sectors, incorporated into standards, regulations and, ultimately, into tender specifications. Take the burgeoning Care sector as a case in point. Medical advances and changing demographics mean that Care will take an increasing share of national budgets throughout the world. We live longer and with greater longevity comes greater frailty. Governments are struggling to meet the challenge this poses and the UK has been rocked by a series of scandals involving maltreatment of elderly residents in care homes.

Much of this provision is delivered under contract by private businesses, and is monitored and regulated by site inspections. Clearly this hasn't worked. The obvious recourse for regulators is to look to use technology as a smart, cost-effective way of supplementing on-site visits: that means remote, continuous monitoring and, in turn, interconnectedness and secure communications systems.

Third, and this follows on from the previous point, we often talk of the public and private sectors as discrete entities. The reality is that we live in a mixed economy and will continue to do so. *Provision* of many goods and services at national and local levels is funded by taxpayers. *Delivery* is managed through a combination of government agencies and outsourcing to private businesses and, increasingly, to a third sector of charities and social enterprises: organisations that are run in a businesslike way, but have a clearly-stated social purpose. The balance of providers depends largely on where you happen to live, but overall there is a drive for governments in many countries to reduce public sector headcounts and devolve service delivery to others. The example we used in Part I, of a new school commissioned by government, featured a mix of potential providers, but all held to the same contractual standards. Just because you are one type of contractor, it doesn't mean that the rules of competition won't apply.

The big take-out is that *everyone* will need to raise their game to stay *in* the game. Big businesses, which have traditionally waited for the major contracts to come their way, cannot afford to be complacent. The data in mid-2017 showed that strategic suppliers – that is, a small number of major firms – accounted for less than 5% by value of UK public procurement contracts, as government sought to redress the balance between corporates and the SMEs who make up 99% of UK businesses. For their part, smaller businesses will need to step up to the mark, to ensure that they meet the requirements to get on to the Approved Supplier lists.

The Good News

IF YOU'VE READ all this with a growing feeling of despondency, here's some good news. While writing winning bids isn't going to get easier [though we hope we've been of some help], change is always accompanied by opportunity. We'll end on three themes that offer some grounds for optimism: innovation, continuous improvement and strategy.

In Part III we urged you to capture and record past examples of innovative and fresh approaches, in support of your bidding. Experience suggests this kind of evidence can be a decisive factor in winning many kinds of tender. Bear in mind, however, the hackneyed but valid distinction between features and benefits. The seller is naturally inclined to promote features, especially when it comes to projects that depend heavily on technology or technical skill. The customer buys benefits: what will your bells and whistles do *for me*? The new imperatives we've described above will reinforce the significance of genuine innovation, i.e. that which provides benefits for the buyer. If you can show how you will deliver the project faster, cheaper or more effectively, without compromising the quality of the outcome, your submission is going to go to the top of the pile. New and compelling ideas will be rewarded, as will be investment in the skill base required to make them a reality. If you offer up the same, tired formulaic approach, don't be surprised when your calls are not returned.

In Part III we also identified continuous improvement as a source of competitive advantage. This tends to sit as a matter of course alongside a culture of innovation, reflecting the same essential mindset. By definition, innovators are dissatisfied with the status quo and strive to do better. Given their opportunity, they create a culture of continuous improvement. Billionaire inventor Sir James Dyson reportedly made some 1000 variants of his revolutionary vacuum cleaner before he felt ready to go to market.

Take, for instance, the basic need for private accommodation. Britain desperately requires more housing. The backlog of unbuilt stock has been increasing for years. Traditional housebuilding methods take many months, even years, to deliver new housing and often to minimally acceptable standards. Modular factory construction of units that can be assembled in days on site is an alternative that is growing in recognition and, moreover, in public acceptance. Perception is changing: as providers have invested continually in reducing manufacturing costs, improving cycle times and raising quality, so *prefabs* are no longer automatically seen as the cheap, second-rate option. In December 2016 Asian construction giant China National Building Material company committed to £2.5bn of funding for six new modular construction factories in the UK, in partnership with housing association Your Housing Group and renewable energy specialist WElink. Designs are being supplied by Barcelona Housing Systems, which has pioneered this approach in Spain. Internationalisation works both ways. Expect to see traditional UK housebuilders successfully challenged by the new entrants.

The message for bidders? Nurture your innovators and fresh thinkers. If you have a scarcity of such people in your organisation, grow your own or recruit them.

Finally, we return to where we started in Part I, at the beginning of this book: the importance of strategy and, with it, focus. In too many businesses, strategy is their Achilles' heel: it's a concept they pay lip service to, but there's no substance behind the words. If you probe, you quickly find that there's no real sense of where the business is heading or how it's going to get there. Measuring the organisation by its deeds, rather than its words, reveals that the slightest setback produces an abandonment of the declared strategy, and a desperate rush to secure any kind of work. It doesn't take long for disenchantment and cynicism to set in as a consequence. The innovators and the fresh thinkers who will secure the future will head for the door. A really great corporate culture takes a long time to build and no time at all to destroy.

To restate a point we made earlier, without a clear idea of direction it's a matter of chance whether you'll end up where you'd like to get to. A business that can demonstrate clarity of purpose, reflected in its bidding strategy, and communicated to its workforce, will stand out from its peers.

At the end of the day, it's all about winning!

APPENDICES

Appendix 1

Appendix 1.1: Calculation of Bid Volumes

Assumptions

Base information derived from European Union & UK Data

Bid information related to GDP

Calculations for Rest of World based on a comparable GDP effect

Bids Per $GDP is adjusted against Europe $GDP

Ratios Used:

European Union + UK

	100%	Expressions of Interest
	25	Average No. of Main Organisations involved in PQQs
	2	Average No. of Specialist Organisations involved in PQQs
	6	Average No. of Main Organisations involved in ITTs
Public Bids Above OJEU Threshold	6	Average No. of Specialist Organisations involved in ITTs
	5	Average No. of Main Tenders involved in BAFOs
	3	Average No. of Main Organisations involved in BAFOs
	2	Average No. of Specialist Organisations involved in BAFOs

Public Bids Below OJEU Threshold	2	Multiplying Factor x Above OJEU Threshold Bid Volumes to indicate Below Threshold Bid Volumes
	6	Average No. of Main Organisations involved in ITTs
	2	Average No. of Specialist Organisations involved in ITTs
Private Bids	4	Multiplying Factor x Above OJEU Threshold Bid Volumes to indicate Private Bid Volumes
	4	Average No. of Main Organisations involved in ITTs
	2	Average No. of Specialist Organisations involved in ITTs

Ratios Used:

Rest of the World

Main Public Bids	Various	Public Bid Volumes related to GDP and based on Public $Bids Per GDP Indicated on this Summary Page
	20	Average No. of Main Organisations involved in PQQs/EOIs
	6	Average No. of Main Organisations involved in ITTs
	6	Average No. of Specialist Organisations involved in ITTs
Small Public Bids	2	Multiplying Factor x Above Main Public Bid Volumes to indicate Small Public Bid Volumes
	6	Average No. of Main Organisations involved in ITTs
	2	Average No. of Specialist Organisations involved in ITTs

Private Bids	6	Multiplying Factor x Above OJEU Threshold Bid Volumes to indicate Private Bid Volumes
	4	Average No. of Main Organisations involved in ITTs
	2	Average No. of Specialist Organisations involved in ITTs

Appendix 1.2: Bid/No Bid Template

Project/Bid Lead:			
Lead Author:			
Bid Writer:			
Key Contributor(s):			
Lead Reviewer:			
Reviewer(s):			
Review Dates:	1st Draft (PINK):	2nd Draft (RED):	Final:

STRENGTHS / WIN THEMES SPECIFIC TO QUESTION AND WHY APPLICABLE

To be informed through our conversations with, and understanding of, the client. Win themes should be client specific, and provide a benefit to the client.

Win Theme 1	Win Theme 2	Win Theme 3	Win Theme 4	Win Theme 5

CLIENT REQUIREMENTS

(Consider relevant client strategic objectives, information gained through conversations and RFP documents, e.g. Value for Money, Innovation, BIM Strategy, etc.)

ROLES AND RESPONSIBILITIES

(Team structure / organogram required to deliver. WHO is responsible for delivery, credentials, experience and WHY them?)

KEY RISKS, OPPORTUNITIES AND PROPOSED MITIGATIONS

What is the client worried about, and how can we reassure the client that we will manage accordingly, mitigating/reducing the risk?

INNOVATIONS

(Present and in the future)

EVIDENCE AND WHY RELEVANT

IMAGES

(Link to folder of selected images to use throughout the bid)

KEY WORDS / LANGUAGE

(Adopt client's language, key words to emphasise win theme)

OTHER

(Any other notes and considerations, possible Technical Queries required, additional resource requirement, etc.)

PROMISES AND COMMITMENTS

(Expand as required)

Question No.	Question Description	Description of Promise or Commitment	Reason for requesting	Date submitted	Approved?

RFP Section/Chapter:		**Common Theme** *(if any):*	
Question No:			
Page Limit:			
Score / Weighting:			
Question:			
Sub-Question(s) *(if any):*			
Reference Documents *(Other Bid documents to read, or any documents within public domain worth consulting in relation to this question):*			

DELIVERABLES FOR THIS QUESTION

(Expand as required. Input / Work required from internal/external team in order to complete question. Identify Deliverable, Person Responsible and Date of Delivery):

Deliverable	Person Responsible	Date of Deliverable
(e.g. provide names for projects to be referenced within response)		

TOPICS TO BE COVERED IN THE ANSWER

(Consider Global/Common Themes, Benefit to the client statement, WHAT we're doing, HOW we're doing it, and WHY). Section will likely form introduction to our response:

ROLES AND RESPONSIBILITIES RELATED TO THIS RESPONSE

(Team structure / organogram required to deliver. WHO is responsible for delivery, credentials, experience and WHY them?):

KEY RISKS, OPPORTUNITIES AND PROPOSED MITIGATIONS RELATED TO THIS QUESTION

What is the client worried about, and how can we reassure the client that we will manage accordingly, mitigating/reducing the risk?

INNOVATIONS RELATED TO THIS QUESTION

(Present and in the future):

EVIDENCE AND WHY RELEVANT TO THIS QUESTION:

• *Link evidence to sub-questions where relevant*

• *How does evidence align with the client's strategic objectives?*

GRAPHICS REQUIREMENTS FOR THIS QUESTION

(To aid final formatting and Graphic Designer Team. Indicate likely graphic(s) and level of support required):

TABLE REQUIREMENTS FOR THIS QUESTION

(To aid final formatting. Indicate likely table requirements and proposed content):

OTHER

(Any other notes and considerations, possible Technical Queries required, additional resource requirement, etc.):

PRINCIPAL ELEMENTS OF THE QUESTION AND ESTIMATED PAGE ALLOWANCE

(Will form heading / subheading structure of final response, expand section to include required content under each sub-question):

Headings to be used through text

• Bullet point contents to be included in the content

Text and Sound Bites for the Response:

Appendix 2

Appendix 2.1 – Bid and Tender Checklist

We advise running a check of each key item before submitting the bid. You may wish to add to our standard list to suit your particular tender. If you have a particularly large tender, you may need to carry out this exercise at the end of each section or before passing it as completed to your line manager. It provides you with the opportunity to run through the document with a fresh pair of eyes, picking up items you may have missed.

It is also a good idea to include a count of how many times you have used your organisation's name versus how many times you have used the name of your target client. Your bid may meet with a cool reception if you have mentioned the client only a handful of times and yet have referenced yourselves throughout. And, yes, that does happen.

Repeating your organisation's name multiple times also may lead the bid reviewer to suspect the use of boilerplate bid writing: submissions in which answers have been cut and pasted from one tender to another. As we've already stressed, clients are looking for responses that are bespoke to the project, and *cut and dumpers* typically don't include the client's name to avoid the risk of leaving the last target client's name in the next tender! Tendering organisations are alert to this and it's the fast track to early elimination. If you are running the bid, watch out for your team doing this and thereby compromising your submission.

Bid and Tender Checklist

Contract Number:	
Client Name:	
Bid Name:	
Question:	
Writer initials:	
Action	
Save and Version Control?	
Author's Name Check?	
Question at the top of the page?	
Marking criteria included?	
Word count/page limit included?	
Flash words highlighted?	
Headings added?	
Read the document?	
Does it answer the Question?	
Relevance check?	
Sense check?	
Acronym check?	
No defraying language: • Would • Should • May • Might • Seek	
Is there a sell?	
Is the Client's name included?	
Correct Client Name?	
Repetition?	
Is there any Evidence?	
Is there any Added Value?	
Are there any Client Benefits?	
Type of Contract?	

Bid and Tender Checklist

Tense check?	
Flash word check?	
Similar words check: • Complaint/compliant • First/fist • Form/From • Contact/Contract • Angle/Angel • Manager/Manger	
Capitalisation check: • Job titles • Names • Works • Risks • Stakeholders • [Type of work]	
Spell check?	
Grammar check?	
Word/Page count check (ensuring the whole allowance is used and it is compliant)?	
Justified Text?	
Format check: • Page Layout • Narrow Margins • Line spacing • Logos • Bullet points	
Font/text Size Check?	
Colour/Highlight Removal?	
Comment check?	

Appendix 2.2: BAFO Case Study

Introduction

When making the decision to enter a BAFO (Best and Final Offer) tender scenario, a bidder has to be mindful of the additional costs to their organisation. Participation in a BAFO requires huge continuity of effort from the selected team members and the redoubling of that effort every time the goalposts move!

However, as can be seen from the calculations below, the prize can be transformational for both the target client and the bid winner[s].

The case study describes a BAFO framework tender which resulted in the bidder being awarded a partner place on the framework. The key learning from a BAFO tender is to balance the potential size of the prize against the effort that is required over an extended period to achieve success.

Bid information

➺ **Client** – Social housing landlord.

➺ **Bid opportunity** – Refurbishment of social housing in central London.

➺ **Contract size** – £20m per annum x five years x two selected organisations = £200m or £100m per successful organisation.

➺ **Bid scenario** – Based on a sample large model project and small model project.

➺ **Contract award** – Based on: quality 60% and price 40%.

➺ **Bidding organisation** – 14-week actual bid working period:

   ➺ Pre-qualification questionnaire (PQQ) – four-week period.

   ➺ Invitation to tender (ITT) – six-week period.

   ➺ BAFO – four-week period.

➺ **Client organisation** – 52-week overall procurement period:

- ➳ Preparation Period – 26 weeks.

- ➳ PQQ – four weeks.

- ➳ Break period – four weeks.

- ➳ ITT – six weeks.

- ➳ ITT Review – three weeks.

- ➳ Break Period – two weeks.

- ➳ BAFO – four weeks.

- ➳ Tender Result – one week.

- ➳ Standstill or *Alcatel* period – ten days.[6]

Bidding strategy

Pre-qualification questionnaire stage (PQQ)

- ➳ Four-week period x 30 organisations.

- ➳ Mandatory attendance at a client meeting to help bidders understand client organisation, including vision, mission and strategy, plus tender objectives and outcomes.

- ➳ Shortlist of eight organisations, selected for next stage with a gap of four weeks.

- ➳ All bidding organisations informed of decision.

Invitation to tender stage (ITT)

- ➳ Six-week period for submissions from shortlisted eight bidders.

---

6 A standstill period of a minimum of ten days, during which other organisations – typically unsuccessful bidders – have a statutory right to challenge the award of a contract tendered via the *Official Journal of the European Union*. So named after two landmark court cases.

➤ Tender documents issued, with a one-week examination period prior to a mandatory attendance at a series of client workshops with stakeholders over two days.

➤ Client meets bidding organisations' operational teams.

➤ Q&A session on issued tender documents.

➤ Team behaviour tests undertaken.

ITT review stage

➤ Following the ITT tender submission, a client tender review period of three weeks.

➤ Client clarification requests to bidding organisations.

➤ Further shortlist of four bidding organisations selected for next stage, with a two-week interval between stages.

➤ All bidding organisations informed of decision.

Best and Final Offer stage (BAFO)

➤ Four-week period involving the four shortlisted bidding organisations.

➤ Preparatory work – client specified the basis for the stage including:

➤ Detailed examination of the model projects to extract:

   ➤ Efficiencies.

   ➤ Value for money.

   ➤ Innovation.

   ➤ Partnership working.

Bidding organisations attend:

➤ One initial interview with all stakeholders.

➤ Two individual exploratory sessions.

➤ Two group exploratory sessions.

BAFO outcomes

The client then had to make critical decisions regarding any amendments to the original ITT conditions, to embrace all agreed changes. These included:

➵ A change in the works order priority.

➵ A shortened programme period.

➵ Use of client property for site accommodation.

➵ Linking together of other programmes of works.

➵ Proposal for sharing resources between partner organisations.

➵ A change of replacement windows specification.

➵ Tender documents reissued with changes.

Bidding organisations submitted a BAFO with further qualifications. In their final submission, our bidder proposed an initial 5% reduction from the original ITT submission, with potential to achieve a further 10% over the life of the contract: an anticipated overall saving on the original submission of a minimum of £20m!

Tender result

➵ Ten-day period.

➵ The client chose two bidding organisations to partner with, and issued an award notice.

➵ On expiry of the *Alcatel* period, the two successful organisations became the selected partners, one being our bidder.

Overall bidding costs

Costs to the tendering organisation – the client:

➵ Framework planning = £20,000.

➵ Internal meetings = £20,000.

➤ Stakeholder meetings = £30,000.

➤ Professional consultant fees = £80,000.

➤ Bid documents = £40,000.

➤ PQQ bid adjudication = £60,000.

➤ ITT adjudication = £80,000.

➤ BAFO adjudication costs = £20,000.

➤ **Total client costs = £350,000.**

Total potential savings [on our bidder's part of the project] = £20m over five years.

Estimated bidding costs to participating organisations:

➤ PQQ stage = £15,000 x 30 organisations = £450,000.

➤ ITT stage = £50,000 x eight organisations = £400,000.

➤ BAFO stage = £20,000 x four organisations = £80,000.

➤ **Total industry cost = £930,000.**

Total cost to the successful bidding organisation [our bidder] = £85,000

Total workload prize for our bidder = £100m over five years!

Appendix 3

General Data Protection Regulation

The **General Data Protection Regulation [GDPR]** (Regulation (EU) 2016/679) is a regulation by which the European Parliament, the Council of the European Union and the European Commission intend to strengthen and unify data protection for all individuals within the European Union (EU). It also addresses the export of personal data outside the EU. The primary objectives of the GDPR are to give control back to citizens and residents over their personal data and to simplify the regulatory environment for international business by unifying the regulation within the EU. When the GDPR takes effect, it will replace the data protection directive (officially Directive 95/46/EC) from 1995. The regulation was adopted on 27 April 2016. It becomes enforceable from 25 May 2018 after a two-year transition period and, unlike a directive, it does not require any enabling legislation to be passed by national governments and is thus directly binding and applicable.

Appendix 4

Key Lessons from the Collapse of Carillion

In mid-January 2018, shortly before this book was due to go to press, the UK's second-biggest provider of outsourced services to government went bust, leaving thousands of unpaid subcontractors in its wake. The latest information we have seen suggests that unsecured creditors are likely to receive less than one penny in the pound – perhaps even nothing at all.

We followed this story closely as it unfolded. Even though the dust has yet to settle finally, there are evidently lessons to be learned: both specific lessons regarding bidding and contracting, and more general lessons about managing business risk.

Lesson One: If it looks too good to be true, it probably is. Carillion historically reported net margins above the average for its sector. Construction and its allied services is a low margin business. If a company is consistently outperforming its peers, there has to be a good reason. In reality, Carillion was not widely regarded as an exemplary business, with widespread complaints from subcontractors about late payment and excessive on-site bureaucracy leading to project overruns.

Lesson Two: Turnover is vanity, profit is sanity, cashflow is reality. This old business maxim is as true today as ever it was. Carillion was heavily focused on the top line, and had grown through aggressive acquisition of other businesses. It seems clear, however, that what Carillion was buying was not so much other firms as their portfolio of contracts and future business pipelines. This strategy increased the strain on their cashflow and piled on the debt to unsustainable levels.

Lesson Three: You can operate sustainably on low margins, but only if the cashflow works in your favour. Take the supermarket sector, for comparison. This traditionally operates with margins comparable to construction, but generates positive cashflow. The customer pays at the checkout, but the suppliers of the goods purchased have to wait 60 or 90 days for payment. The supermarket has its working capital funded up-front. A major factor in the delayed payments to Carillion's subcontractors was the time-lag the company faced in getting paid by its own customers.

Lesson Four: Too many eggs in the wrong basket. Carillion's cashflow problems were compounded by its heavy reliance on government, a notoriously slow paymaster. Presumably banks were prepared to provide interim funding on the basis that public sector customers do not go bust, and so will pay eventually, but the costs of bank debt have to be serviced and the business was inherently vulnerable to changes in interest rates.

Lesson Five: Diversifying the business portfolio does not necessarily equal reducing business risk. Its acquisition of other businesses took Carillion into other areas. On the face of it, this seems a good idea, especially for a large organisation. If, for example, the demand for new hospitals stalls, it may be balanced by an upsurge in demand for new schools, and vice versa. A delay in starts on new builds may be countered by a continuing need for maintenance and the supply of services. However, if the profile of the customers is broadly the same – i.e., they are all slow payers – the financial risk to the business has been raised, not reduced.

Lesson Six: Management capability has to keep pace with growth. Carillion's expansion and diversification seems to have outstripped its ability to manage an ever-more complex business. By all accounts, the depth and breadth of management in the company were insufficient to keep up with the demands of the business and the key competences of project management and engineering expertise were in short supply. The financial engineering that appears to have taken precedence over civil engineering surfaced in too many projects under the control of accountants who lacked the appropriate skills.

What could and should Carillion have done differently?

Hindsight is, of course, a wonderful thing. But the implications of the lessons are clear enough. For us, three things pre-eminently stand out. First, going for growth does not in itself constitute a business strategy. In fact, the bigger you are, the harder you fall, and a company with half the turnover and greatly-improved cash balances would have been inherently more sustainable. Second, far too little attention was paid to managing the business risks that increase with growing size and complexity. Indeed, the financial statements that have emerged suggest that senior management is likely to have progressively lost sight of the basics in the struggle to make sense of the balance sheet and trading position. And third, management *bandwidth* was insufficient to handle the operating challenges created by Carillion's overstretch.

Many readers of this book will be in the position of being subcontractors to main contractors. For them, this sorry episode reinforces, in our view, key messages we have emphasised in the main text:

➡ Be clear about your strengths and align these with your bidding strategy.

➡ Do not fall into the trap of bidding for anything and everything, but subject candidate bids to a rigorous Bid/No Bid screening process: never, ever, find yourself saddled with the winner's curse of landing a project you wish you had never tendered for.

➡ Prioritise wherever possible tenders with a strong Quality emphasis: successful bidders are less likely to be squeezed constantly on price.

➡ When conducting your background research, ensure that you do basic due diligence on the target client, their financial health, their payment terms, and their reputation in the market for dealing with subcontractors. It is better to walk away than find yourself burdened with costs that you have little or no chance of recovering.

About Bidwriting.com

Bidwriting.com is a specialist bid writing consultancy formed ten years ago, to work with organisations all over the world, and across many different sectors.

Bidwriting Academy is our dedicated division that provides training in bid writing skills from basic through to advanced levels. It has extended to delivering in-house training for clients looking to create depth and breadth of skills across their businesses.

Bidwriting Analytics is a specialist company that provides marketing analysis to support fact-based decision-making.

For further information, please visit our main website:
www.bidwriting.com